Measuring the Statutory and Regulatory Constraints on DoD Acquisition

Research Design for an Empirical Study

Jeffrey A. Drezner, Raj Raman, Irv Blickstein,
John Ablard, Melissa A. Bradley, Brent Eastwood,
Maria Falvo, Dikla Gavrieli, Monica Hertzman,
Darryl Lenhardt, Megan McKernan

Prepared for the Office of the Secretary of Defense

NATIONAL DEFENSE RESEARCH INSTITUTE

The research described in this report was prepared for the Office of the Secretary of Defense (OSD). The research was conducted in the RAND National Defense Research Institute, a federally funded research and development center sponsored by the Office of the Secretary of Defense, the Joint Staff, the Unified Combatant Commands, the Department of the Navy, the Marine Corps, the defense agencies, and the defense Intelligence Community under Contract DASW01-01-C-0004.

Library of Congress Cataloging-in-Publication Data

Measuring the statutory and regulatory constraints on DoD acquisition: research design for an empirical study / Jeffrey A. Drezner ... [et al.].
    p. cm.
    Includes bibliographical references.
    ISBN-13: 978-0-8330-3967-5 (pbk. : alk. paper)
    1. United States. Dept. of Defense—Procurement—Costs—Study and teaching. 2. United States. Dept. of Defense—Rules and practice—Study and teaching. I. Drezner, Jeffrey A.

UC263.M42 2006
355.6'2120973—dc22

                    2006022427

The RAND Corporation is a nonprofit research organization providing objective analysis and effective solutions that address the challenges facing the public and private sectors around the world. RAND's publications do not necessarily reflect the opinions of its research clients and sponsors.

RAND® is a registered trademark.

Published 2006 by the RAND Corporation
1776 Main Street, P.O. Box 2138, Santa Monica, CA 90407-2138
1200 South Hayes Street, Arlington, VA 22202-5050
4570 Fifth Avenue, Suite 600, Pittsburgh, PA 15213
RAND URL: http://www.rand.org/
To order RAND documents or to obtain additional information, contact
Distribution Services: Telephone: (310) 451-7002;
Fax: (310) 451-6915; Email: order@rand.org

Preface

Over the past two decades, the Department of Defense (DoD) has been striving to make acquisition-related statutes and regulations less burdensome to program offices. While many studies have focused on the "costs" of doing business with DoD, few have attempted to quantify the actual cost of compliance.

The Office of the Under Secretary of Defense for Acquisition, Technology, and Logistics (OUSD[AT&L]) asked the RAND Corporation's National Defense Research Institute (NDRI) to quantify the impact of statutes and regulations that are burdensome to program offices. The study's focus on program offices was the result of the many anecdotes from program managers about how burdensome some statutes and regulations are, and how that burden translates into adverse consequences for program outcomes. RAND approached the overall research project by dividing it into a set of successive efforts, namely (1) identifying which statutes and regulations are burdensome, (2) developing and validating a methodology to quantify that burden, (3) collecting quantifiable information from program offices, and (4) suggesting relief measures to alleviate the burdensome tasks where possible. This report discusses the first two research efforts in detail.

This report should be of interest to Program Offices, Program Executive Offices within the Services, Office of the Secretary of Defense (OSD), Congress, and contractors with an interest in doing business with DoD.

This research was sponsored by the Office of the Under Secretary of Defense for Acquisition, Technology, and Logistics and conducted within the Acquisition and Technology Policy Center of the RAND National Defense Research Institute, a federally funded research and development center sponsored by the Office of the Secretary of Defense, the Joint Staff, the Unified Combatant Commands, the Department of the Navy, the Marine Corps, the defense agencies, and the defense Intelligence Community.

For more information on RAND's Acquisition and Technology Policy Center, contact the Director, Philip Antón. He can be reached by e-mail at atpc-director@rand.org; by phone at 310-393-0411, extension 7798; or by mail at the RAND Corporation, 1776 Main Street, Santa Monica, California 90407-2138. More information about RAND is available at www.rand.org.

Contents

Tables

Summary

Over the past two decades, multiple studies have attempted to estimate the cost to major weapon system programs of complying with acquisition-related statutes and regulations. Most studies investigated the cost of compliance only at the contractor level, though program offices, the Services, and OSD would also incur such costs. A majority of these studies defined compliance cost as the additional cost of doing business with DoD. Despite substantial research in this area, few studies based their findings on actual, measured costs. Instead, most based their results on anecdote rather than the systematic collection of empirical data.

Compliance with statutes and regulations is imbedded in the working culture of the DoD organization. Personnel are taught to comply during their acquisition training, and they do not know another way of doing business. A two-star Program Executive Officer described the acquisition system as a sandbox that he knows and understands, and opined that it was not in his interest to spend what little time he had to manage his programs fighting to lower the height of the walls of that sandbox, even if that would make his and his staff's jobs easier. The high degree to which compliance is institutionalized in a culture and in a set of processes creates an inherent difficulty in quantifying the cost of that compliance.

This research focuses on costs at the government program office level primarily because it is program managers and their staff who complain that compliance with some statutes or regulations is burdensome, and that burden translates into adverse outcomes in terms of cost, schedule, and performance. One way of capturing actual costs at the government program office level is to track the actual labor hours spent by program office staff complying with a certain statute or regulation. Linking these compliance activities to program deliverables that are in the critical path shows their effect on cost and schedule outcomes. Capturing such costs would provide a richer understanding of the actual, full cost of compliance at the program level.

Research Objectives

In response to long-standing complaints by weapon system program managers, OUSD(AT&L) requested that RAND empirically evaluate the cost of compliance with statutes and regulations at the program office level.[1] RAND designed a study to identify specific instances in which compliance with acquisition-related legislation or regulations has led to an identifiable penalty, such as time lost, additional cost incurred, a loss of system capability, additional demands on critical staff, or some other imposition on the program office. If no effects can be proven through the documentation process, we will identify that as well. If significant effects are found, we will develop alternative concepts for mitigating those constraints.

The study addresses the following questions:

- Which statutes and regulations are currently considered most burdensome at the program office level?
- How can we capture the *actual* cost of compliance with burdensome statutes and regulations?
- What is the cost of compliance at the program office level, and how much of that can be attributed to burdensome statutes and regulations?
- What measures can be taken to reduce this burden?

The first two questions constitute the first phase of this research effort, summarized in this document. This report discusses the development and pilot testing of a data collection tool capable of quantifying the impact of statutes and regulations at the program office level.

A separate report will address the second pair of research questions, including the data collection, analysis, and mitigation activities.

Research Approach

Interviews were conducted with current and former OSD personnel, program office staff (including Flag Officers), and senior Service officials in an attempt to identify which statutes and regulations are currently the most burdensome. Individuals in different organizations tended to define "burdensome" in ways that corresponded to their roles in the acquisition process and the perspectives of their organizations. In its simplest form, however, "burden" is defined as the perceived time and effort spent on a compliance task that appears to add little or no value to the acquisition process. The interviews were open ended in nature, with the objective of recording what these senior officials considered to be the most burdensome statutes and regulations. The responses were then categorized into several statutory and regulatory areas, and the areas most frequently cited as burdensome were identified as candidates for further study.

A Web-based data collection tool was developed and pilot tested in the E-2C and Apache program offices over two two-week data collection periods. The objectives of the pilot-phase testing were to ensure that

---

[1] A Major Defense Acquisition Program (MDAP) is managed by a government program office with responsibility for planning and executing the program. A program office is staffed by a combination of military, civilian, and contractor support personnel.

- program office personnel understood what we were asking for and could provide that information,
- we properly captured the key compliance activities in each area,
- the tool had no major software problems, and
- the Web-based format was instructional and easy to use.

Concurrently, an extensive literature review was conducted of past studies that identified statutory and regulatory constraints, quantified their impact, and described the mechanisms through which these impacts occurred in defense acquisition programs. While most studies looked at the cost to contractors of doing business with DoD, very few were able to quantify actual costs, leading to a high degree of uncertainty in the estimates. Results of the 1994 Coopers and Lybrand study quantifying the cost of compliance across several statutes and regulations have been by far the most widely received in the DoD community. This study calculated the cost of compliance with DoD-unique statutes and regulations at 18 percent; that is, systems purchased by DoD included an 18-percent cost premium due to compliance activities. However, these results are heavily based on estimates provided by experts at ten contractor sites.

The literature review also revealed that acquisition reform initiatives have been proposed and implemented on a continuous basis over the past several decades in an effort to reduce statutory and regulatory burdens. Broadly speaking, the same basic set of problems was identified and the same set of solutions proposed, including adopting commercial products and processes and streamlining decisionmaking within DoD. The specific content of these initiatives has varied over the years, depending on such factors as the political and budgetary environment. Many recommendations made by previous studies have been implemented and yet do not appear to have had the desired effect. This is partly due to the difficulty in quantifying the savings expected from such changes in an environment in which statutes and regulations are deeply embedded in the organizational culture. As a result, quantifying the savings from not complying with statutes and regulations, or the "path not taken," is extremely challenging.

Identification of Burdensome Areas Through Interviews

Our interviews resulted in a list of areas that are perceived as burdensome to one or more of the following organizations: the prime contractor, the program office, and Service and OSD oversight organizations. The statements below reflect the perceptions of the officials we interviewed. RAND did not attempt to validate whether the perception of a burden in fact indicated an actual burden. Our research is designed to understand whether the perception of a burden, itself, is in fact a burden with consequences to program outcomes. The results of our analysis will be documented in a separate report.

- The Clinger-Cohen Act requires compliance reporting, perceived as burdensome, that focuses on understanding the definition of information technology (IT) and how it applies to weapon systems.

- The Core Law and 50-50 Rule require that 50 percent of DoD-wide maintenance workload be conducted at government facilities, thereby forcing the program offices to spend resources ensuring that this requirement is met.
- Reprogramming activities associated with moving program funds between accounts are seen as burdensome. Different accounts have different rules associated with expenditures and tracking of funds.
- Cost reporting requirements levied upon the contractors lead to costs incurred by the program office.
- Program status reports, such as the Selected Acquisition Report (SAR), Defense Acquisition Executive Summary (DAES), and Unit Cost Report (UCR) contain redundant information that increases reporting burden.
- The effectiveness of overarching integrated product teams (OIPTs) is reduced when the participating members do not have the authority to make decisions on behalf of the program, thereby necessitating additional briefings to senior decisionmakers.
- The Bayh-Dole Act requires, among other things, that contractors provide intellectual property rights to the government and increases government oversight requirements for managing the information.
- Some operational testing activities are perceived as mandated by the Director, Operational Test and Evaluation (DOT&E), and are considered redundant by the program offices. This is perceived to be driven primarily by the requirement that DOT&E act as an independent examiner.
- Live fire test and evaluation (LFT&E) of a weapon system is perceived as expensive, and it requires the program office staff to generate waivers if they believe that certain types of live fire testing are unnecessary.
- The Competition in Contracting Act (CICA) results in lengthy Request for Proposal (RFP) efforts in which the government solicits proposals from several contractors to foster full and open competition.
- The Truth in Negotiations Act (TINA) inhibits the participation of commercial firms that are reluctant to spend the necessary resources to disclose information on their financial accounting structures.
- DoD has routinely encouraged procurement of commercial off-the-shelf (COTS) items, but these bring costs associated with modification and issues related to availability and long-term support.
- DoD's complex regulatory environment represents prohibitive costs to small business ventures relative to those of the prime contractors that are well versed in the statutes and regulations of the DoD organization. This potentially reduces the pool of contractors and subcontractors available to contribute to a program.
- The Buy American Act forces the government to procure items made in the United States in an age of multinational corporations, which is considered burdensome and stifling to innovation.
- Program offices typically pay for incorporating jointness and system of systems concepts in acquisition programs, while the Services and the DoD organization as a whole reap

the benefits in the form of performance enhancements through interoperability. Joint programs tend to be more difficult to manage, often involving approvals from more than one Service.

- OSD policy on the incorporation of the Joint Tactical Radio System (JTRS) in all systems currently in production requires waivers to be submitted every year, even though the radio will not be available until at least 2008.[2] These annual submissions are therefore considered redundant and burdensome.

Officials at all levels had anecdotes describing how a particular statute or regulation affected a program, but no one was willing to provide an empirical estimate of those consequences in terms of cost or schedule. Additionally, most officials used terms such as "time spent" or "level of effort" to describe how the perceived burdens manifested at the program level.

Table S.1 lists these perceived burden areas and indicates the organizational level affected. Different organizational levels are affected differently by the same statute or regulation. Note that most of the items on the list would entail some degree of compliance activity at the program office level.

Based on the results of our interviews, the following categories were the most common burden areas across the different organizations and individuals we spoke with:

- Clinger-Cohen Act (CCA)
- Core Law and 50-50 Rule
- program status reporting (PSR)
- program planning and budgeting (PPB)
- technical data[3]
- testing.

CCA activities relate to the management of IT embedded in weapon systems. The Core Law and 50-50 Rule entail planning and reporting activities associated with logistics. PSR deals with all activities pertaining to reporting the status of a program at the program office level. These activities include the DAES, SAR, UCR, and monthly status reports to the Service, as well as OIPT and Defense Acquisition Board (DAB) review processes. Many different statutes and regulations drive the compliance activities in PSR, including the DoD 5000 series, which governs program management. PPB pertains to all budget-related activities performed by a program, from providing input to the DoD budget process to moving funds among accounts and "what if" exercises performed in response to a real or proposed change. These programmatic changes may be caused by changes in law, directed by OSD, the Services, or Congress. The PPB area is also driven by a multitude of statutes and regulations,

---

[2] Since our initial interviews, the JTRS program has experienced technical difficulties that will push back the availability of the radio.

[3] This category was later dropped from the study as a result of feedback during the pilot test.

Table S.1
Statutes and Regulations Perceived as Burdensome

Statute or Regulation	Burden				Included in Category
	OSD	Service	Program Office	Contractor	
Clinger-Cohen Act	X	X	X	X	CCA
Core Law and 50-50 Rule		X	X	X	Core Law and 50-50 Rule
Reprogramming activities			X	X	PPB
Cost reporting			X	X	PSR
Program status reporting			X	X	PSR
OIPT process		X	X	X	PSR
Bayh-Dole Act	X	X	X	X	Technical data
Operational testing activites (DOT&E)		X	X	X	Testing
LFT&E		X	X	X	Testing
CICA			X	X	Not included
TINA			X	X	Not included
COTS			X		Not included
Costs to small business		X	X	X	Not included
Buy American Act	X	X	X	X	Not included
Jointness and system of systems		X	X	X	Not included
JTRS waivers		X	X		Not included

as well as institutional processes within DoD. Testing pertains to all related reporting activities, including the Test and Evaluation Master Plan (TEMP) and Operational and Live Fire Test reports, as well as interaction between the program office and Service and the OSD test organizations.

Table S.1 indicates whether each of the statutes and regulations identified as burdensome during the interviews was included in these five areas, and if so, in which area. Note that while activities associated with these five areas are perceived as burdensome to program offices, compliance activities are also often perceived as burdensome to other organizations. This study focuses only on the costs of compliance at the program office level.

General Observations from Interviews and Literature Review

Our in-depth review of past studies, combined with information from our interviews, led us to the following general observations:

- Policy and process design, as well as how those policies and processes are actually implemented, has the greatest effect on perceived burden. Few officials at any level disagree with the intent of specific policies; it is the way in which one tries to achieve those objectives that produces a perception of burden.
- The time spent complying with statutes and regulations is dominated by attempts to "work the process" to ensure that the program is executed as well as possible. This often translates as creative ways of shielding the program from any substantial adverse consequences for program outcomes related to compliance activities.
- The Services differ in both culture and in how statutes and regulations are interpreted, leading to different implementation approaches and, hence, different "costs."
- Most program office personnel are generally aware of the legal basis for their statutory or regulatory compliance activities, as well as the motivational basis (intent of the statute or regulation). However, these are not foremost in their minds as they execute the program: They are simply doing their jobs. This indicates how institutionalized these acquisition processes have become.
- The literature seems to suggest that consequences, if any, are relatively small. Program managers typically incorporate the time it takes to comply with rules and regulations in their program plans. With the exception of major milestones, such routine compliance activities are never on the critical path.

We treat these observations as hypotheses to be tested as part of this research effort.

Developing a Web-Based Data Collection Process

To better understand how program office officials perceive statutory and regulatory burden and to generate empirical data on compliance costs at the weapon system program offices, we developed a unique approach that combines both qualitative and quantitative methods. Based on our reading of the statutes and regulations in a particular area, we identified the specific activities necessary for compliance in that area. We listed these activities, along with appropriate definitions, on a Web site, our Web-based data collection tool. Individuals within program offices whose responsibilities included relevant compliance activities were asked to record on our Web site on a biweekly basis the time they spent on such activities. The reported hours constitute the empirical element of our approach.

We also provided space (blank text boxes) that participants could use to provide comments associated with the hours they reported against a particular activity. These comments provided important contextual information that was used in interpreting the results of the analysis. RAND researchers reviewed these comments after each reporting period was complete and contacted specific individuals directly in order to obtain additional information related to the activity. Additionally, we provided a space for participants to make general observations about their compliance activities, their perceptions of what was burdensome, and suggestions for addressing perceived problems.

The research design required participating program office personnel to report both the quantitative and qualitative information over a 12-month period. This allowed us to capture fluctuations in compliance activities associated with periodic and annual events. Our research design also included frequent site visits to participating program offices to review their input and to ask for their help in validating and interpreting the results. This follow-up approach was designed to document, whenever possible, the impact of a specific compliance activity on program cost and/or schedule through delays in meeting target dates for certain deliverables.

Pilot Phase Testing

We successfully tested the Web-based data collection tool at the E-2C and Apache program offices during March 2004. Feedback from program office personnel greatly improved the tool itself, and demonstrated that individuals in the program office could associate the time they spend on specific activities with specific statutes or regulations. The pilot test results also indicated that a significant initial effort by the program office was required in order to identify the personnel who should be enrolled in the study and that the participants would need to use the tool multiple times before becoming familiar with it. Nevertheless, program office management and staff demonstrated a willingness and ability to participate in the study.

Next Steps

We will implement this Web-based approach across eight program offices, including E-2C and Apache, for a period of one year to capture the variations within an annual budget cycle. Program office personnel will be interviewed periodically to follow up on key burdensome areas that may affect program cost and/or schedule. Such effects should be identifiable through marginal cost increases or through delays in meeting specific product delivery dates. This should provide a richer understanding of the actual cost of compliance at the program office level.

Our goal is to identify specific instances in which compliance with acquisition-related legislation or regulations has led to an identifiable penalty, such as program delays, additional cost incurred, loss of system capability, additional demands on critical staff, or some other imposition on the program office. If no effects can be proven through the documentation process, we will identify that as well. If significant effects are found, we will develop alternative concepts for mitigating those constraints.

After the completion of the data collection period, we will work with relevant OSD offices to help mitigate any significant burdens that are identified in the analysis. This might include changes to existing policies or developing alternatives to existing laws. Over the long run, the existence of empirical, quantitative data may help DoD decisionmakers design policies and processes that minimize both the perceived and actual costs of compliance.

Acknowledgments

We would like to extend our gratitude and appreciation to the program office, Service, OSD, and industry officials who gave their time and insights in support of this research.

Special thanks are due to CAPT Robert Labelle, program manager for E-2C and COL Ralph Pallotta, program manager for Apache, for agreeing to allow their program offices to participate in our pilot test. Lola Scott at E-2C and Carole Lang at Apache provided great support by coordinating their programs' participation and being liaisons between RAND researchers and the participating programs' office personnel. And finally, we greatly appreciate the efforts of all the personnel from each program office who not only tested our data collection tool but also provided many useful suggestions for refining it.

Any errors are the responsibility of the authors.

Acronyms

ACAT	Acquisition Category
AFOTEC	Air Force Operational Test and Evaluation Center
APB	Acquisition Program Baseline
AR	Office of Acquisition Reform
ASR	Acquisition Strategy Report
ATEC	Army Test and Evaluation Command
BLRIP	beyond low rate initial production
CAIG	Cost Analysis Improvement Group
CAIV	Cost as an Independent Variable
CARS	Cost Analysis Reporting System
CAS	Cost Accounting Standards
CCA	Clinger-Cohen Act
CCDR	Contractor Cost Data Report
CDD	Capability Development Document
C4I	command, control, communications, computers, and intelligence
C4ISP	command, control, communications, computers, and intelligence support plan
CICA	Competition in Contracting Act
CIO	chief information officer
COI	critical operational issue
COMOPTEVFOR	Navy Commander, Operational Test and Evaluation Force
COTS	commercial off-the-shelf
CPD	Capability Production Document
DAB	Defense Acquisition Board
DAES	Defense Acquisition Executive Summary
DCAA	Defense Contract Audit Agency
DCMAO	Defense Contract Management Area Operations

DCMC	Defense Contract Management Command
DoD	Department of Defense
DOT&E	Director, Operational Test and Evaluation
DT	developmental testing
DT&E	developmental test and evaluation
FAR	Federal Acquisition Regulation
FARA	Federal Acquisition Reform Act of 1996
FASA	Federal Acquisition Streamlining Act
FOIA	Freedom of Information Act
FRP&D	full rate production and deployment
FRPDR	Full Rate Production Decision Review
FY	fiscal year
G&A	general and administrative
GAO	General Accounting Office, now Government Accountability Office
GIG	Global Information Grid
IA	Information Assurance
ICD	Initial Capabilities Document
IIPT	integrated initial product team
IOT&E	initial operational test and evaluation
IPT	integrated product team
IT	information technology
ITA	Information Technology Architecture
ITMRA	Information Technology Management Reform Act of 1996
JTA	Joint Technical Architecture
JTRS	Joint Tactical Radio System
LFT&E	live fire test and evaluation
LRIP	low rate initial production
MCOTEA	Marine Corps Operational Test and Evaluation Activity
MDAP	Major Defense Acquisition Program
MILCON	military construction
MILSPEC	military specification
MMAS	Material Management and Accounting System
NDAA	National Defense Authorization Act
NDRI	National Defense Research Institute
O&M	operations and maintenance

OIPT	overarching integrated product team
OSD	Office of the Secretary of Defense
OT	operational testing
OT&E	operational test and evalujation
OTRR	Operational Test Readiness Review
OUSD(AT&L)	Office of the Under Secretary of Defense for Acquisition, Technology, and Logistics
PA&E	Program Analysis and Evaluation
PEO	program executive office
POM	Program Objectives Memorandum
PPB	program planning and budgeting
PSR	program status reporting
R&D	research and development
RDT&E	research, development, testing, and evaluation
RFP	Request for Proposal
SAE	Service Acquisition Executive
SAR	Selected Acquisition Report
SBIR	Small Business Innovative Research
SoS	system of systems
SPI	Single-Process Initiative
T&E	test and evaluation
TDY	temporary duty
TEMP	Test and Evaluation Master Plan
TINA	Truth in Negotiations Act
UCR	Unit Cost Report
USD(AT&L)	Under Secretary of Defense for Acquisition, Technology, and Logistics

CHAPTER ONE

Introduction

Background and Motivation

Commissions and organizations have tried to improve the defense acquisition process for more than 50 years, and studies addressing the topic have fairly consistently identified the same set of problems and proposed the same solutions. In 1986, the Packard Commission recognized that legislative and regulatory constraints on the Department of Defense (DoD) acquisition process and personnel affect the efficiency and effectiveness of the acquisition process.[1] In 1992, DoD created the Office of Acquisition Reform (AR) to be the focal point for identifying changes that could improve both process efficiency and outcomes while maintaining a necessary level of accountability and oversight. Many of the changes proposed either through past studies or AR recommendations have been implemented. For example:

- The modifications to DoD acquisition policy and implementation guidance (DoD Directive 5000.1 and Instruction 5000.2) and the associated requirements generation process (CJCSI 3170.01) that occurred in 2003 resulted in a significant restructuring of the acquisition process.
- Programmatic changes such as the imposition of the now-defunct program stability wedge, which enhanced the Services' ability to maintain stable funding profiles for programs, and use of the Cost Analysis Improvement Group (CAIG) cost estimate for Acquisition Category (ACAT) I programs were implemented to ensure full funding.
- Changes in law, such as the Clinger-Cohen Act (changes in the management of information technology) and the Federal Acquisition Streamlining Act (FASA) (changes to the Federal Acquisition Regulations), were recommended and approved by Congress.

Nevertheless, the perceived problems surrounding defense acquisition have changed little over the years.[2] Part of the problem may stem from a "regulatory pendulum" that responds to fraud, waste, and abuse with increased regulation and then swings back in response to complaints of regulatory burden.[3] Laws and regulations became tighter in the late 1980s in response

---

[1] Packard Commission (1986).

[2] See, for instance, Rich, Dews, and Batten (1986) and Defense Policy Panel and Acquisition Panel, House of Representatives Committee on Armed Forces (1988).

[3] Hanks et al. (2005).

to several highly visible examples of fraud earlier in that decade. The 1990s saw increased acquisition reform activity, mostly targeted at removing those regulatory constraints.[4] Recent examples of abuse will likely result in tighter rules in the near future.[5] For now, however, it is widely believed by the DoD acquisition community (including decisionmakers, program managers, and analysts) that DoD acquisition programs continue to operate under a series of statutory and regulatory constraints that stifle innovation, impair productivity, and result in increased costs and schedule delays.

Costs and Benefits of Statutes and Regulations

Most acquisition officials agree that statutory and regulatory constraints adversely affect program outcomes, but they are nevertheless unable to provide credible estimates of the magnitude of those effects. Past studies have produced widely varying and generally unsatisfying results: It is very difficult to demonstrate the effects of these constraints because compliance is deeply embedded in acquisition processes and institutions, and, generally, the effects cannot be identified separately. Acquisition managers recognize both the statutory and regulatory constraints (though they cannot always distinguish between them) and adjust the resulting inefficient process. Relevant data on the cost of compliance are not collected during the course of routine program execution, and acquisition officials have little basis for making credible estimates of consequences.

The lack of any empirical analysis of the costs (and benefits) of statutory and regulatory compliance makes targeted change difficult, resulting in extreme swings of the regulatory pendulum. In April 2003, DoD submitted to Congress the Defense Transformation for the 21st Century Act, which contained Office of the Secretary of Defense (OSD) proposals for changing personnel management, the acquisition process, and selected administrative and budgetary processes within OSD.[6] The last 88 pages of the 207-page document contain a list of 183 congressionally mandated reporting requirements affecting DoD; following each requirement is a proposal to either repeal or to change it, as well as a short justification for the proposal. Table 1.1 categorizes the main justifications.[7] While Congress eventually enacted some of the legislative proposals, it passed few of the proposals to repeal or change specific reporting requirements, in part because DoD could not demonstrate that the costs of these reports were higher than the perceived benefits. With few exceptions, there were no quantitative estimates of the costs of the reporting requirement, and for the few estimates provided, there was no substantiation.

---

[4] Hanks et al. (2005) identified 63 distinct acquisition reform initiatives in the 1990s, all but one oriented at improving acquisition process efficiency.

[5] U.S. Department of Defense (2005).

[6] Transmittal letter and attachment from the General Council of the Department of Defense, April 10, 2003 (U.S. Department of Defense, 2003).

[7] Although the act proposed changes to 183 reporting requirements, each proposal may contain any or all of the justifications listed in the table.

Table 1.1
DoD Justifications for Repealing Reporting Requirements

Justification	Frequency
Unnecessary	66
Overly burdensome	64
Redundant	51
Limited utility	43
Obsolete	25
High cost	13
Harmful to national security	1
Adds delay	1

Despite the lack of hard evidence, compliance with statutes and regulations clearly entails "costs." Such costs manifest as reporting requirements, coordination and approval processes, schedule delays during the wait for approval, the need for additional personnel dedicated exclusively to statutory and regulatory compliance, and the need for senior-level program officials to focus on such issues rather than on the management of their programs.

At the same time, statutes and regulations also entail "benefits," otherwise they would not have been enacted. Benefits include oversight and accountability; standardization and formalization of decision processes; prevention of fraud, waste, and abuse; ensuring fairness; and providing guidance for inexperienced personnel. One might debate the merits of such benefits and whether they are worth the costs, but the proponents of statutes and regulations clearly thought they were addressing a problem.

Reporting requirements provide a good example of the costs and benefits of regulation. The need to provide reports is generally assessed as a cost by the organization responsible for reporting if it has to expend resources without receiving any obvious benefits. In general, the costs of program status reporting accrue at the program level, while the benefits accrue at higher organizational levels.

At the program office level, monthly status reports are provided to the Program Executive Officer or Service Acquisition Executive (SAE); the quarterly Defense Acquisition Executive Summary (DAES) to the Under Secretary of Defense for Acquisition, Technology, and Logistics (USD[AT&L]); and the Selected Acquisition Report (SAR) to Congress. The program office bears the costs (program management resources, time spent by program personnel) of generating these reports, but does not generally see any direct benefit to its program. As a recipient of the DAES, the Office of the Under Secretary of Defense for Acquisition, Technology, and Logistics (OUSD[AT&L]) uses it to monitor the health of Major Defense Acquisition Programs (MDAPs) across DoD. Additionally, OSD Program Analysis and Evaluation (PA&E) benefits from the DAES and SAR as analytical tools to track current and historical performance while using the information for estimating and projecting future impacts. Congress uses the SAR to monitor program status and to force the identification and resolution of problems. The program office pays for these reports through staff time and contractor support, but the beneficiaries are OSD and Congress. It is therefore understandable that the program office may view these reports as burdensome while the other organizations do not.

The program office does benefit from some reports, however. It needs monthly status reports, such as the Contractor Funds Status Report (CFSR), Cost Schedule Status Report (CSSR), and Cost Performance Report (CPR), as part of its Earned Value Management (EVM) system of monitoring program status. Semiannual reports, such as the Contractor Cost Data Report (CCDR), also allow the program to make estimates and projections for any program modifications based on historical expenditure patterns. Although the prime contractors prepare these reports, a portion of the program office budget funds their preparation. This is a situation in which the program office pays for, as well as benefits from, the reporting requirements.

Research Objectives

A crucial gap clearly exists between the perceived impacts and documented effects of statutes and regulations on the defense acquisition process. Our research attempts to fill the gap and provide an empirical analysis of the effects of statutory and regulatory constraints on outcomes at the program office level.

To a large extent, our approach is experimental. RAND and others have analyzed specific issues, including Other Transaction Authority, special-access programs, and pilot programs in the context of a case study approach, but there has been no truly empirical, systematic study.

The problem is that statutory and regulatory constraints are deeply embedded in existing procedures, making it difficult to separate the consequences of legislative or regulatory actions from the many other controls and events that affect program cost, schedule, and performance outcomes. Additionally, in a government context, there will always be some regulation and oversight because other measures, such as profit, are not sufficient or are inappropriate. The optimal research design would be to define a program's "path not taken" (i.e., the program as it would be without legislative or regulatory constraints) and compare a program executed with and without statutory and regulatory constraints. Unfortunately, the complexity of the regulatory environment does not allow us to credibly define and assess the path not taken. This conundrum presents a difficult research challenge. Thus, our research involves an important methodological component: demonstrating an approach to identify and quantify the effects of statutes and regulations on acquisition programs.

Our goal is to identify specific instances in which compliance with acquisition-related legislation or regulations has led to a specific, identifiable penalty. That penalty might be time lost, additional cost incurred, loss of system capability, additional demands on critical staff, or some other imposition on the program office. If no effects can be proven through the documentation process, we will identify that as well. If significant effects are found, we will develop alternative concepts for mitigating those constraints. This includes working with OSD staff to either change existing policy or develop legislative alternatives to existing law. Over the long run, the existence of even limited empirical data may help policymakers design policies and processes that achieve expected benefits at minimal perceived and actual costs.

Approach

Our research was conducted over a period of two years and was divided into three interrelated phases:

Phase 1: Research Design

To be confident that the research will succeed, we spent significant time designing the overall research approach and the data collection protocol in particular. This phase involved discussions with officials throughout the DoD acquisition community to identify statutes and regulations perceived as burdensome and to develop metrics to capture the effects of those statutes and regulations. This phase also included the selection of candidate programs for participation and the development and test (through a pilot test conducted at the beginning of Phase 2) of a Web-based data collection protocol.

An important research task in this phase consisted of a comprehensive review of existing studies and databases. We assessed studies of the legislative and regulatory constraints on acquisition processes both to assemble the substantive results from prior research on this topic and to draw methodological lessons from that prior analysis experience. This task provided the foundation for the development of our own research design and will provide the appropriate background and context for interpreting the results from the primary data collection.

Phase 2: Data Collection

This phase involved implementing the data collection protocol developed in Phase 1, beginning with a pilot test period in which the data collection protocol was fielded at two program offices. We assessed the results of the pilot test and incorporated lessons into a revised instrument prior to fielding it more widely. Full fielding of the protocol subsequent to the pilot test period was envisioned to take approximately 14 months (to capture a full annual cycle of program activities). During this stage, we worked closely with the participating program offices to ensure that the data collection was accurate and only minimally disruptive to the primary mission of the program. We periodically reviewed and summarized the data being collected in order to understand emerging patterns and results and to inform any reform proposals emerging from OSD or Service Acquisition Officials.

Phase 2 also included several related research activities that enabled better insight and more confident interpretation of the data collected through the protocol. These activities included compiling abbreviated case studies of the participating programs, collecting and analyzing additional program data relating to changes in program schedule or scope, and conducting periodic discussions with program officials to identify the consequences of the activities we were tracking. Additionally, we held discussions with Service and OSD officials responsible for the statutory and regulatory areas of interest.

Because of the need for primary data collection, this research required the support of OSD and Service acquisition leadership, as well as the full participation of the programs using the data protocol.

Phase 3: Analysis and Implementation

After the 14-month data collection activity, we performed a comprehensive analysis of the data collected in Phase 2. This task was intended to yield solid, persuasive evidence linking specific statutes or regulations to specific effects on specific programs, or to demonstrate that such evidence does not exist or is inconsequential. Should specific constraints be identified, we would assist OSD in drafting proposals to change the statutory or regulatory basis of acquisition-related processes.

Organization of This Report

This is an interim report documenting the initial research design phase of the study, as well as the pilot test conducted at the beginning of Phase 2. We felt that publishing a separate document on methodology would allow us to provide more detail on our approach, which would allow readers to better assess the validity of our approach and assist in interpreting results. The full fielding of the data collection protocol, the analysis, and the results are to be published separately.

Chapter Two presents a brief history of acquisition reform as well as a review of relevant acquisition reform literature focused on attempts to identify, measure, or mitigate the impact of statutory and regulatory constraints on acquisition programs. This provides important context and places our study firmly within the decades of acquisition reform and policy analysis. Chapter Three summarizes the results of our initial round of discussions with officials in the acquisition community at the OSD, Service, program executive office (PEO), and program office levels. These interviews helped us to identify a set of statutes and regulations for further examination. Chapter Four describes in detail our research approach, including the statutory and regulatory areas chosen for further analysis, the design of the Web-based data collection tool, and the results of the pilot test of that tool. The final chapter summarizes our observations to date.

The appendixes contain additional details about our approach and focus. Appendix A contains the user manual developed for our Web-based data collection tool. Appendix B contains screenshots of that tool. Appendix C provides additional information on the five statutory and regulatory areas selected for analysis.

CHAPTER TWO

A Review of Acquisition Reform Literature and History

Acquisition reform has been a goal for decades. There have been many initiatives since the mid-1980s, but few have brought about measurable change. One of the main challenges researchers have faced has been the inability to quantify and assess how changes in policy and the regulatory environment affect programs. Most studies rely on anecdotal evidence, leading to some uncertainty regarding the reliability of their conclusions and the broader applicability of those conclusions outside the specific anecdotal case. In periods of increasing oversight, the government may benefit from increased accountability and a reduction of waste, fraud, and abuse, but with a potentially increased cost premium and reluctance among firms to do business with DoD. Periods of increased flexibility are thought to spur innovation and improve efficiency, but with the potential for increased waste, fraud, and abuse. These two opposing trends create a pendulum that constantly swings between regulation and deregulation.

This chapter presents the results of a literature review that focused on the statutory and regulatory environment surrounding the management of defense acquisition programs. Of particular interest to us were studies and analyses that

- identify problems or constraints that the legal or regulatory environment creates for programs,
- quantify the impact of these constraints on acquisition programs, and
- describe the mechanism through which such impacts occur.

The majority of the studies on acquisition reform are not empirical, consider only costs and not benefits, and include no follow-up concerning the implementation of regulations. Most address the problems that defense-specific laws and regulations create for program execution and outcomes; many also identify and describe the mechanisms through which these problems manifest.[1] Relatively few attempt to quantify the consequences of the regulatory environment on program execution and outcomes.

We primarily consider studies that attempted to quantify the costs of statutory and regulatory compliance to the acquisition process. For these studies, we closely examine the objectives, approaches, results, and challenges that flow from quantifying the cost of constraints that are deeply embedded in existing procedures. Some studies led to reform initiatives and

---

[1] See Hanks et al (2005). See also Defense Policy Panel and Acquisition Policy Panel (1988).

changes in statutes and regulations. For these, we examine the extent to which implementation has resulted in cost savings. Lastly, we address the lack of follow-up on implementation of reforms and the trends that have created the "pendulum effect" that has the acquisition community swinging from regulation to deregulation. The discussion that follows provides the foundation upon which we base our own research design.

Recent Studies

In the late 1980s and throughout the 1990s, research organizations, industry groups, Congress, and DoD, among others, produced hundreds of studies on acquisition reform. These included commission reports, position papers, historical analyses, and numerous micro-level studies focusing on some specific aspect of the defense acquisition process, selected weapon programs, or Service-centered concerns. Many of these studies have had a significant impact on reforms and contain valuable insights into the problems inherent in the acquisition process. Although the majority of these studies are qualitative, they are consistent in their underlying themes, problems cited, and solutions proposed.

Congressional studies, although often qualitative, found that the burden of regulatory controls imposed through the DoD acquisition system is an important factor in the decline of the defense industrial base.[2] A 1992 congressional study found that "[the] Defense Department provisions requiring compliance with Government Cost Accounting Standards and the Truth in Negotiations Act are serious impediments to commercial companies wishing to sell to the department."[3] Since these studies found that many of the regulations that impose the most burdensome controls are specifically mandated by statute,[4] they call for legislative rather than regulatory reform.

Another group of studies recommended the increased use of less-costly commercial products, whose quality is often comparable to products built according to DoD specifications.[5] In the past, high-tech commercial products have been pushing the state of the art and changing so quickly that the DoD military specification (MILSPEC) system was unable to keep pace. Although these studies never answered the questions of how much could be saved in the long run and exactly how to measure such savings, in the mid- to late 1990s, Congress passed reforms to alleviate constraints and enable the use of "commercial" products and practices.

Some studies focused on delays in program deliverables rather than on costs. One such study found that oversight does not cause delays, but rather that the delays are merely a symp-

---

[2] U.S. Congress, Office of Technology Assessment (1991); U.S. Department of Defense, Defense Systems Management College (1993).

[3] U.S. Congresss, House of Representatives Committee on Armed Services (1992).

[4] U.S. Department of Defense, Defense Systems Management College (1993).

[5] Lorell, Lowell, et al. (2000); Anderson (1997).

tom of other problems.[6] A 1983 analysis of the milestone review process found that the process is effective but not efficient, and further concluded that the process did not directly affect the overall length of a program.[7]

Many studies have attempted to show that contractor compliance with statutes and regulations imposes a significant cost premium on government-procured items. Table 2.1 presents various studies' estimates of the DoD regulatory cost premium; that is, what the DoD pays contractors to cover the added cost of complying with DoD-specific statutes and regulations.[8] The cost premium can also be viewed as the potential savings available from acquisition reform. Although all of the studies listed in Table 2.1 attempt to calculate a DoD-wide cost premium, each study differs in its approach, the manner in which it defines cost, and the political environment at the time of the study. Additionally, the unique program or groups of programs studied often influence the results and make the conclusions very difficult to generalize across all programs within DoD. Attempts to do so have resulted in estimates that government regulation increases costs anywhere from 5 to 200 percent.[9] The very wide range reflects the high level of uncertainty in such estimates. Although studies have found the cost savings potential to vary significantly, the underlying premise is always the same: DoD statutes and regulations impose a significant cost premium on DoD procurement. A RAND report that examined many such studies from 1986 to 1992 found that most of the studies in the late 1980s and early 1990s that were able to estimate cost savings potential used very limited data and differing methodologies, and although they were able to derive percent potential cost savings, the overall analyses are qualitative.[10]

The specific focuses and methodologies of the studies listed in Table 2.1 vary significantly, and thus the results are not directly comparable. Most "empirical" estimates confront significant methodological challenges and, consequently, are actually based on expert opinion, anecdotal information, or projections derived from commercial analogies that may or may not be appropriate.[11] Thus, these numbers should be examined cautiously. Furthermore, the unit of analysis differs across these studies: Some studies analyze firms while others analyze programs or program budgets. In the next section, we examine the most "empirically credible" studies in more detail.

Interestingly, we found few studies with empirical estimates of compliance costs after the late 1990s. Those we did find focused on estimating the savings from reform; these studies are addressed in Table 2.3.

---

[6] Institute for Defense Analysis (1991).

[7] Acker (1983).

[8] Specifically, the DoD regulatory cost premium refers to all additional costs DoD pays to contractors in order to cover the cost of complying with DoD-unique statutes and regulations beyond the cost in a purely commercial environment.

[9] U.S. Congress, Office of Technology Assessment (1989).

[10] Lorell and Graser (2001).

[11] Lorell and Graser (2001).

Table 2.1
Estimates of the DoD Regulatory and Oversight Cost Premium

Study	Year	Unit of Analysis	Estimated DoD Cost Premium or Potential Cost Savings (%)
Honeywell, *Defense Acquisition Improvement Study*	1986	Internal study of 20 programs	13
Smith et al., *A Preliminary Perspective on Regulatory Activities and Effects in Weapons Acquisition*, RAND	1988	Total program costs	5–10
U.S. Congress, Office of Technology Assessment, *Holding the Edge: Maintaining the Defense Techology Base*	1989	Total DoD acquisition budget	10–50
CSIS, *Integrating Commercial and Military Technologies for National Security*	1991	Cost premium on identical items	30
Carnegie Commission, *A Radical Reform of the Defense Acquisition System*	1992	Total DoD acquisition budget	40
ADPA, *Doing Business with DoD—The Cost Premium*	1992	Product cost questionnaires; internal studies	30–50
OUSD, Acquisition and Technology, *Report of the Defense Science Board Task Force on Acquisition Reform*	1993	Government/industry panel approach	20
NORCOM, *Activity-Based Cost Analysis of Cost of DoD Requirements and Cost of Capacity*	1994	Third-party data collection; testing Coopers & Lybrand's results; no new raw data	27
Coopers & Lybrand with TASC, Inc., *The DoD Regulatory Cost Premium*	1994	10 contractor sites	18
OUSD, Acquisition and Technology, Acquisition Reform Senior Steering Group, DoD Regulatory Cost Premium Working Group	1996	Program analysis of Coopers & Lybrand's top 24 cost drivers	6.3
GAO, *Acquisition Reform: Efforts to Reduce the Cost to Manage and Oversee DoD Contracts*, DoD Reducing Oversight Costs Reinvention Laboratory study	1996	Program analysis of Coopers & Lybrand's top 10 cost drivers	6.1
Office of the Assistant Secretary of the Air Force, Acquisition, *Acquisition Reform Success Story: Wind Corrected Munitions Dispenser*	1997	Contractor data requirements lists only (cost savings in research and development)	3.5

Responses to the Earlier Studies

The findings of the studies conducted in the late 1980s helped DoD to prepare a workable set of recommended changes to acquisition law. The National Defense Authorization Act for fiscal year (FY) 1991 established the Section 800 Panel,[12] the purpose of which was to review and propose ways to streamline existing DoD acquisition laws and processes that some of the

---

[12] Section 800 refers to the section of the FY 1991 National Defense Authorization Act containing language establishing the panel.

studies identified as problematic. The group's subsequent report was instrumental in laying the groundwork for several pieces of major procurement reform legislation passed in the early 1990s.[13]

The Section 800 Panel identified more than 800 provisions of law that had some relationship to DoD acquisition, although detailed reviews later reduced this number to just over 600. Of the laws reviewed by the panel, almost 300 were recommended for repeal, deletion, or amendment. The changes recommended for these statutes would result in a streamlined system of acquisition laws that would be more easily understood and implemented. It also recommended significant legislative changes to improve DoD's access to commercial technologies and emphasized the need to simplify contract management for both DoD and its suppliers.

In 1994, efforts to create a "government that works better and costs less"[14] brought about a revision of more than 225 statutory rules and a swing of the pendulum from regulation to deregulation. Based on recommendations of the Section 800 Panel, the Federal Acquisition Streamlining Act (FASA) significantly changed how the government does business. This act encouraged federal agencies to buy commercial off-the-shelf products, and it simplified government procedures for procuring those products. Some of the key provisions of FASA include raising the threshold for waiving many statutes governing defense procurement and streamlining the bid-protest process to prevent costly delays that could result when contractors protest procurement awards. Other provisions raised the cap to allow bidding defense contractors to bypass special accounting systems requirements and avoid providing lengthy cost and pricing data to the government.

Acquisition studies continued to proliferate, however, and the cost premiums cited continued to grow. In the early 1990s, the Principal Deputy for Acquisition, U.S. Army Materiel Command (AMC), directed NORCOM, a private consulting firm, to undertake a study with the goal of determining the cost of Army contractors' compliance with DoD regulations. NORCOM's study applied activity-based costing to data collected from six U.S. Army contractors, most of whom specialized in military-unique items. In its final report, dated May 1994, NORCOM estimated that the weighted average DoD regulatory cost premium amounted to 27 percent.[15]

A "Landmark" Study

More than any other study, however, the December 1994 study conducted by Coopers & Lybrand, The *DoD Regulatory Cost Premium: A Quantitative Assessment*, is regarded as a landmark in acquisition reform research. The Coopers & Lybrand study provided what many consider a uniquely empirical analysis of the burden imposed by the statutory and regulatory environment surrounding DoD acquisition. Previous case studies relating to the impact of the

---

[13] U.S. Department of Defense, Defense Systems Management College (1993).

[14] Vice President Gore presented the Federal Acquisition Streamlining Act to President Clinton in 1993 as part of his effort to create a "government that works better and costs less."

[15] NORCOM (1994).

DoD acquisition environment on contractors' costs focused solely on estimating the total DoD cost premium. The Coopers & Lybrand study attempted to tie compliance costs to specific DoD-unique statutory and regulatory requirements.[16]

The report proved to be highly influential and remains the most cited document in acquisition reform because it is widely considered to be the first truly objective assessment of the DoD regulatory cost premium. Coopers & Lybrand analyzed ten contractor sites representing $7.2 billion in military sales and spent the equivalent of 25 man-months in the field. The researchers interviewed 1,000 contractor personnel (executives, cost center managers, and other key workers), completed 500 worksheets, documented 5,000 business activities, and assessed 120 cost drivers. At the request of then–Secretary of Defense William Perry, Coopers & Lybrand also used findings from the Section 800 Panel report in the study. In all of the literature on acquisition reform following the study, the most important estimates of the DoD regulatory and oversight compliance cost premium are based on data derived from Coopers & Lybrand. For this reason, we discuss this particular study in more detail than the others.

Methodology

The Coopers & Lybrand project team used value-added costs as the cost base for its assessment.[17] It defined the DoD cost premium as equal to the contractors' compliance costs divided by the contractors' value-added costs:[18]

$$\text{DoD cost premium (\%)} = \frac{\text{contractor compliance costs (\$)}}{\text{value-added costs (\$)}}.$$

After arriving at a company site, the project team reviewed the firm's organizational structure with input from company personnel and identified cost centers (the lowest level of an organization for which costs are budgeted or collected: primary business functions such as finance, quality assurance, and operations). After grouping cost centers into business functions, the project team interviewed cost center managers. The team excluded from their site assessment those cost centers supporting only commercial operations but did include indirect cost centers supporting both DoD and commercial operations. Coopers & Lybrand used cost

---

[16] Coopers & Lybrand with TASC, Inc. (1994).

[17] Such costs are equal to total costs less the costs of material purchases, including subcontracts. Coopers & Lybrand used value-added as the basis for measuring regulatory cost impacts because prime contractors use the practice of "flowing down" most contract terms and conditions to their major subcontractors. The project team adjusted the value-added cost base slightly by excluding profits and, when applicable, corporate general and administrative (G&A) allocations. Profits were excluded because of the firms' reluctance to provide this information and because, in the defense industry, profits are driven largely by costs. Corporate G&A allocations were excluded because there are no means to assess regulatory impacts at the corporate level when conducting site assessments at the division or facility level.

[18] Using total costs rather than value-added costs in the denominator would result in double-counting of material costs (material purchases of the prime contractor are largely value-added costs of subcontractors and suppliers) and thus would lead to an understatement of the regulatory cost impact.

allocation formulas approved by the Defense Contract Audit Agency (DCAA) to remove from defense costs those expenses related to the support of the commercial side of the contractor's business.

To allocate the 1994 budgeted expenses properly, and to identify those activities that are impacted by DoD oversight and regulation, the project team developed a hierarchical "process model" documenting all the cost center's processes, subprocesses, and activities. Estimates generated from interviews determined the cost impact on those activities should the regulation and oversight "disappear." Cost center managers were asked to estimate the cost impact on specific activities if best commercial practices were substituted for all DoD regulation and oversight (assuming characteristics and performance requirements of DoD-purchased items do not change). They were also asked to compare their current practices with best commercial practices, prevailing practices in the contractor's commercial operations, and practices utilized in direct military sales to foreign governments. Cost center personnel were asked to provide appropriate qualitative information and to make suggestions as to how DoD might reduce compliance costs while preserving appropriate government accountability. After examining all cost centers in a given function, the project team consolidated the interview results into a summary worksheet for the functional area and provided results to the appropriate function managers for review and concurrence.

Results

The Coopers & Lybrand project team found an average DoD regulatory cost premium of 18 percent of value-added costs. This figure represents a straight average of the site assessment results from the ten facilities. The study concluded that the DoD regulatory environment imposes a substantial cost premium throughout the defense sector that is ultimately absorbed by DoD in the form of increased unit costs for military equipment and services.

The top three drivers account for almost 25 percent of the total DoD regulatory cost premium, and half of the total regulatory cost impact is concentrated in ten key areas. The results suggest that DoD could achieve significant benefits from concentrating its reform efforts on a relatively small number of high-leverage regulatory areas that impose significant compliance costs throughout the defense sector, regardless of industry, tier position, or other factors. The top ten cost drivers and their cost impacts are listed in the Table 2.2.

The Coopers & Lybrand project team found that DoD was the primary change agent (i.e., DoD could initiate changes without additional authority or outside approval) for eight of the ten top regulatory cost drivers. DoD can play an important role in costs associated with the two measures in which Congress has significant involvement (TINA and CAS) by developing and carrying out streamlined, less-intrusive oversight practices.

The study found that the DoD regulatory cost premium—embedded in contractor costs paid for by the government—is significant and that study results are consistent with previous analyses and policy statements. It noted that compliance costs are concentrated in a small number of regulatory/oversight areas, and with the passage of FASA in 1994, many corrective actions could be achieved without further statutory changes. The study concluded that reductions in compliance costs could be achieved over several years.

Table 2.2
Key Cost Drivers, Ten-Site Average

Cost Driver	DoD Cost Premium (%)	% of Total Cost Premium
MIL-Q-9858A	1.7	10.0
Truth in Negotiations Act (TINA)	1.3	7.5
Cost/Schedule Control System	0.9	5.1
Configuration management requirements	0.8	4.9
Contract-specific requirements	0.7	4.3
DCAA/Defense Contract Management Area Operations (DCMAO) interface	0.7	3.9
Cost Accounting Standards (CAS)	0.7	3.8
Material Management and Accounting System (MMAS)	0.6	3.4
Engineering Drawings	0.6	3.3
Government Property Administration	0.5	2.7
Subtotal	8.5	48.9

SOURCE: Coopers & Lybrand with TASC, Inc. (1994).

NOTES: MIL-Q-9858A was a quality assurance MILSPEC. TINA requires certain types of cost and pricing information in support of cost proposals. The Cost/Schedule Control System is a program monitoring and reporting system. CAS refers to all Federal Acquisition Regulation (FAR) Part 30 requirements (Title 48, CFR 99). DCAA/DCMAO captured daily interactions between the contractor and these agencies. MMAS requires certain material management and reporting systems. Engineering drawings and configuration management requirements (MIL-STD-973) refer to various processes used to manage system configuration. Contract-specific requirements is a catch-all category for nonstatutory or regulatory-based requirements that DoD includes in a contract (e.g., additional reporting, testing). The Government Property Administration (FAR Part 45) requires contractors to assume responsibility for maintaining and accounting for government property.

Critique

The numbers in the Coopers & Lybrand study are often referred to as "actual data," whereas in fact they are semi-quantitative estimates based on limited data and a unique methodology. This methodology, though consistently applied, is ultimately subjective in its assessment of the cost consequences of specific statutes and regulations. Although the study concludes with a number (18 percent), it is derived from expert opinion and theoretical analyses, rather than actual (demonstrated) impacts on a program.

The Coopers & Lybrand project team evaluated only the direct costs (e.g., labor) of compliance with DoD regulations at the contractor level. The study concluded that significant savings were potentially achievable through reductions in DoD regulations and oversight without examining the benefits that are associated with the oversight process and without examining the actual cost of implementing reform. The study also did not address costs (or benefits) at the government program office level.

Implementing Study Recommendations and Other Acquisition Reforms

One of the primary reasons the Coopers & Lybrand study is so influential is that its broad conclusion appeared to be confirmed by other studies. The earlier NORCOM study,[19] which estimated that the weighted average DoD regulatory cost premium amounted to 27 percent, was close to the Coopers & Lybrand number of 22 percent regulatory compliance cost for companies that produce military-unique items for DoD.[20] When it came to implementing the changes Coopers & Lybrand recommended, however, it turned out that the estimated savings were much higher than could be realized.

DoD-Initiated Efforts

In response to the Coopers & Lybrand and NORCOM studies, for example, DoD established the Regulatory Cost Premium Working Group to investigate and eliminate the top cost drivers. This team focused on the Coopers & Lybrand study's top 24 cost drivers, which led to a 13.4-percent DoD cost premium, but it concluded that DoD could achieve less than half of those savings. DoD then established the Reducing Oversight Costs Reinvention Laboratory to further investigate the Coopers & Lybrand study's recommendations. Participants included ten contractor sites, the OSD, the Defense Contract Management Command (DCMC), and the DCAA. The Reinvention Lab conducted extensive cost/benefit analyses on reducing oversight and regulatory requirements and reported results in the same categories used in the Coopers & Lybrand study. Five of the ten participants in the Reinvention Lab had prepared their own estimates of the cost impact of the top ten cost drivers at their sites. The results indicated a mere 1.2- to 6.1-percent savings, compared with the Coopers & Lybrand study's estimate of 8.5 percent, and participants had little success in addressing nine of the top ten cost drivers. Almost all projected savings came from adopting commercial standards instead of using MILSPECs.[21]

The complexity of implementation and accounting for benefits are two of the factors that explain the difference between the Coopers & Lybrand study's results and DoD's attempts to actually achieve those savings through changes in policy and process. Nevertheless, cost savings through reductions in the perceived regulatory premium remained a key acquisition reform objective, so in 1994 and 1995, DoD introduced several new acquisition reforms. In June 1994, Secretary Perry introduced a major directive reversing the traditional DoD preference for MILSPECs and focusing instead on performance specifications and commercial standards. Programs now needed special waivers to use MILSPECs, and DoD granted these only in special cases.

In 1995, DoD developed the Single-Process Initiative (SPI), which was intended to reduce the DoD cost premium and to eliminate many of the regulatory barriers identified by

---

[19] NORCOM (1994).

[20] The 22 percent figure in the Coopers & Lybrand study refers to the cost premium incurred by the defense-only firms participating in the study. The more commonly cited 18-percent cost premium figure includes both defense and commercial study participants.

[21] U.S. General Accounting Office (1996, 1997a); Lorell and Graser (2001).

Coopers & Lybrand by promoting block changes to the manufacturing and management requirements of all existing contracts on a facility-wide basis. More than 1,000 changes were made and more than 300 sites were participating by 1998. Upon further examination, however, it is evident that it is difficult to estimate actual savings. DCMC data showed that the SPI resulted in $30.3 million in direct savings to DoD and $472.5 million in extended cost avoidance (over the lifetime of contracts). As a percentage of research, development, testing, and evaluation (RDT&E) budgets, however, the total direct cost savings from SPI amounted to only 0.03 to 0.04 percent.

In May 1995, DoD decided to begin using an integrated product team (IPT) approach when developing and building weapon systems in order to facilitate collaboration between representatives of the contractor, military Service, and OSD. We were unable to find any studies on the relative cost or benefit of this reform.

DoD also attempted to increase the importance of cost as a factor in deciding on the acceptable performance of a weapon system through the Cost as an Independent Variable (CAIV) policy. CAIV forces decisionmakers to consider trading away some system performance to achieve greater cost savings. Under CAIV, program managers must examine a weapon system's entire life cycle, including research and development, production, operation, and support, and its cost patterns and objectives. They must think about cost-related factors such as budgetary resources, unit costs of comparable or fielded systems, mission effectiveness, technology trends, innovative manufacturing techniques, and commercial business practices. Enforcement of CAIV occurs though the authority of oversight organizations; CAIV analyses are reviewed at decision milestones and are required to support cost-performance tradeoff decisions. The challenge to implementing CAIV is the ability to persuade DoD and industry managers to accept less-than-desired performance to preserve or reduce cost. In practice, few programs have made those cost-performance trades.

Congressional Efforts

In 1996, the growing importance of information technology for effective government and the need to further simplify procedures to procure commercial products and services led to even more changes in the acquisition process in areas of competition, commercial items, certification requirements, and the Federal Acquisition Computer Network (FACNET). The Federal Acquisition Reform Act of 1996 (FARA) and the Information Technology Management Reform Act of 1996 (ITMRA) further advanced the changes made by FASA. By eliminating the requirement for certified cost and pricing data for commercial products, FARA aimed to preserve the concept of full and open competition while further reducing barriers to acquiring commercial products.

That year, FASA also directed DoD to reduce its acquisition workforce by 15,000 personnel and to report to Congress on how to implement an overall 25-percent reduction in workforce during the next five years. It also sought to streamline the bid protest process by having all bid protests adjudicated by the General Accounting Office (GAO).

In 1997, Congress focused on integrating the assessments and recommendations of various defense panels charged with assisting the Secretary of Defense in changing the business culture within the department. DoD implemented the Pentagon management and organizational reforms recommended by the Task Force on Defense Reform, including ways to improve business practices within DoD.[22] Secretary Cohen used recommendations to develop Defense Reform Initiatives, including the following:

- reducing the size of the Office of Secretary of Defense, the Joint Staff, and defense agencies from 141,000 to 111,000 staff members
- realigning functions within DoD and consolidating and eliminating duplicate functions
- increasing public-private competition to outsource non–core maintenance and support work
- establishing a senior-level Defense Management Council to monitor compliance.

One of the most significant reforms was changing the DoD 5000 series, which has set acquisition policy since 1969. In 1995, following the passage of the FASA and the push for more-efficient acquisition, then Under Secretary of Defense for Acquisition and Technology, Paul Kaminski, called for the revision of the series to allow more flexibility and, in turn, reform of the system. The original 5000 Series mandated a complicated acquisition process requiring the government to follow specific rules and regulations to ensure that only the highest-quality equipment was purchased. The rewrite of the series in 1997 sought to revise the rules to favor a streamlined acquisition process. The rewrite incorporated new policies and laws, separated mandatory policies from discretionary practices, and integrated for the first time acquisition policies and procedures for both weapon systems and automated information systems. The rewrite not only reduced the volume of internal regulatory guidance, it also reduced the size of the original document from more than 1,000 pages to a mere 160 pages. The DoD 5000 series has since been revised several more times, each in an attempt to simplify the process and better reflect the changing character of technology and industry.[23]

Analyses of Savings

In 1997, at the request of the Service Acquisition Executives and with the endorsement of Secretary Cohen, Coopers & Lybrand published another study to assess the previous four years' implementation of acquisition reform in DoD contracts.

The 1997 Coopers & Lybrand study developed a catalog of 53 acquisition reform changes propagated since January 1993. The research team conducted 430 surveys at ten contractor sites, interviewing program managers, team members, and process managers about the effects of these changes. The survey found that considerable progress has been achieved in implementing acquisition reform in DoD contracts, but that there was a great deal to accomplish to reach full implementation.[24] Industry acknowledged the progress it had made and was committed to working with DoD to affect further change, but implementation was uneven and inconsistent across and within the Services and buying commands. No further follow-up has been conducted on these issues since the 1997 study.

---

[22] See Office of the Under Secretary of Defense (1999).

[23] Ferrara (1996). See also Sylvester and Ferrara (2003).

[24] See Coopers & Lybrand (1997).

Also in 1997, a GAO study of 33 MDAPs predicted that savings from Clinton administration reform efforts (FYs 1996 to 2002) would be negative. This study found that although the programs would experience cost savings because of acquisition reforms, the savings would be offset by cost increases elsewhere or by reinvestment. The study was based on comparisons of overall program budget data and on projections from different fiscal years. It did not differentiate among specific acquisition reform measures nor did it explain how such measures contributed to changes in estimates. At the time the data was collected, radical acquisition reforms were not fully implemented.[25]

Table 2.3 lists some of the studies that examined the effects of acquisition reform implementation.

Table 2.3
Analyses of Acquisition Reform Savings from Implementation

Study	Year	Unit of Analysis	DoD Acquisition Reform Savings (%)
Schank et al., *Analysis of Service-Reported Acquisition Reform Reductions*, RAND	1996	Summary of initial assessment of overall DoD savings for FYs 1995–2001	4.4
Coopers & Lybrand, *Acquisition Reform Implementation*	1997	Assesses implementation of acquisition reform in DoD contracts; industry feedback; 10 contractor sites; project manager interviews	Significant outcomes (on the Coopers & Lybrand scale)
Anderson, *A Study of the Federal Government's Experiences with Commercial Procurement Practices in Major Defense Acquisitions*	1997	Average of 23 MDAPs; savings for FY 1996	4.3
GAO, *Acquisition Reform: DoD Faces Challenges in Reducing Oversight Costs*	1997	Average 33 MDAPs; savings for FYs 1996–2002	–2
GAO, *Acquisition Reform: Effect on Weapon System Funding*	1997	Average 10 MDAPs; savings for FYs 1995–2002	4
Lorell and Graser, *An Overview of Acquisition Reform Cost Savings Estimates*, RAND	2001	Savings from commercial-like programs in terms of research and development (using CAIV); few numbers based on hard data; estimates made pre–product development and production; used 1999 DoD estimates for overall cost savings; lessons from pilot programs	15–35

---

[25] U.S General Accounting Office (1997a).

Pilot Program Experience

Throughout the last decade or so, pilot programs have been established to test whether specific reforms are feasible and produce the expected results. One underlying theme has been whether defense acquisition could be run more like a commercial business. Pilot programs have been launched to determine whether to structure weapon system acquisition programs so that the incentives provided to contractors are more like those found in commercial research and development (R&D) and production programs. The pilot programs aimed to provide incentives to contractors to focus on cost as a primary objective and to use commercial standards, technology, parts, and components.

Very few studies on these programs are based on hard data, and the data that are available suggest that a savings of 15–35 percent in research and development costs may be possible in programs that are fully restructured in a commercial-like manner in accordance with CAIV concepts. The three best-documented cases suggest that savings up to 65 percent are possible, at least in programs with less-complex systems and with high production runs. These cases include the Joint Direct Attack Munition (JDAM), Wind Correct Munitions Dispenser (WCMD), and Joint Air-to-Surface Standoff Missile (JASSM). The reforms demonstrated in these programs have not been widely used, however. Each of these programs is characterized by low technological risk, commercial derivative items, and large production runs. The potential applicability of these reforms to a large, complex weapon system that employs high-risk, cutting-edge technology remains uncertain. The literature does note that some of the most important issues in achieving acquisition reform savings include CAIV, requirements reform, maximizing the use of commercial parts, and true dual-use utilization of production facilities.[26]

Summary Observations

Acquisition reform is not new to DoD, and despite all the reform initiatives, the magnitude of cost savings is uncertain. Neither DoD nor any study we could identify has assessed the costs of the reforms themselves; changing policies and processes entails costs. Additionally, there has been little follow-up on those initiatives that have been implemented to determine whether they worked as expected. This is primarily a result of the fact that compliance costs are difficult to estimate and even more difficult to generalize. The large range of estimates in the literature suggests that a great deal of uncertainty exists because the variety of the data problems is difficult to remedy. Each of the studies discussed is unique in its methodology, unit of analysis, and the political environment of its time. Although each study is unique, the reforms that are later implemented as a result of these studies are surprisingly similar.

For our purposes, several observations can be made from a review of prior studies:

---

[26] Rush (1997); Lorell, Lowell, et al. (2000); Lorell and Graser (2001).

- Acquisition reform has been a continuous activity whose specific content varies as a function of many factors, including political environment, budgetary environment, and preferences regarding the ideal degree of regulation and management control.
- Broadly speaking, the same basic set of problems or challenges has been identified for several decades. These challenges include the need to balance responsibility, authority, and accountability between the program offices that execute a program and the organizations that provide oversight.
- Similarly, the same set of solutions has been proposed to address these challenges, including adopting commercial products and processes and streamlining decisionmaking within the Services and OSD.

Many recommendations made by previous studies have in fact been implemented, but they do not appear to have had the desired effect, or confounding factors and the lack of precise metrics make it difficult to find evidence of the effects of the recommendations.

CHAPTER THREE

Determining Our Research Focus

The long history and dynamic nature of acquisition reform required that we first identify the current and most common statutory and regulatory constraints. Most of the anecdotes about burdensome statutes and regulations and their adverse impact on program outcomes come from program managers and program office staff. The anecdotes often refer to added costs incurred by contractors (and paid for by the government) and the time and effort program managers and their staff spend on compliance activities that are perceived to have little or no value to the program. Previous studies have focused on contractors; we wanted to focus on the government program offices.

To do so, we interviewed senior staff members within the Office of the Under Secretary of Defense for Acquisition, Technology, and Logistics (OUSD[AT&L]); Congressional Research Service (CRS); PEOs; and several Major Defense Acquisition Programs (MDAPs) within DoD. We also interviewed selected defense and commercial contractors. Although we interviewed officials representing all organizational levels in the acquisition process, our goal was to obtain insight into perceived burdensome statutes and regulations at the program office level and to determine how those constraints might be quantified and measured. The specific organizations and officials we interviewed were chosen because they represented key perspectives and stakeholders in the acquisition process.

This chapter presents the results of our interviews with regard to the following questions:

- What statutes and regulations (constraints) are perceived to be most burdensome?
- Why are they perceived as burdensome?
- What are the consequences of compliance activities on program outcomes?

We conclude this chapter by identifying the most frequently mentioned burdensome areas across several program offices. In Chapter Four, we describe an experimental quantification methodology designed to obtain empirical evidence of the effects of compliance activities in these areas on program execution and outcomes.

Identifying Burdensome Statutes and Regulations Through Interviews

Compliance with statutes and regulations is a mandatory and integral part of the DoD organization and is often considered "routine" by program office and oversight officials. Compliance is highly institutionalized in DoD; policy implementation is embedded within traditional acquisition processes and is therefore rarely viewed as a "constraint."

We used interviews to identify statutes and regulations perceived as burdensome. So as not to lead the officials we interviewed, we generally used open-ended questions. We specifically asked which DoD acquisition-related statutes and regulations (including policies, implementation guidance, and processes and procedures) were viewed as burdensome from a program office perspective and requested ideas on how to quantify that burden. The responses suggested that a wide range of acquisition-related laws and regulations are perceived as burdensome, with varying levels of detail on the mechanisms through which such burdens impacted program offices. Different individuals in different organizations tended to define "burdensome" differently based on their roles in the acquisition process and the perspectives of their organizations. *In its simplest form, however, burden is defined as the perceived time and effort spent on a compliance task that appears to add little or no value to the acquisition process.*

The responses regarding measurement and metrics were general in nature and focused on schedule delays affecting the program, labor hours, and related funds spent to comply with a certain statute or regulation. While officials at all levels (OSD, Service, PEO, and program office) had stories to tell about how statutes and regulations affected programs, none was willing to provide even a rough quantitative estimate of an actual cost or schedule consequence.

Interviewees generally concurred that the "costs" of compliance activities often accrue at the program level while "benefits" accrue at higher levels, including the Service staff, OSD, and Congress. They identified a few key factors that contribute to the perception of burden at the program office level, including the level of difficulty and complexity of implementing statutes and regulations in DoD, the experience base and training level of program office personnel, and the work environment associated with each program office and its corresponding Service.

The challenge of implementation begins with interpretation of the statute or regulation at the program office level. When a statute or regulation is ambiguous in its intent or when it can be interpreted in multiple ways, program office personnel find it difficult to identify what needs to be done to satisfy its requirements. For example, in the Clinger-Cohen Act, one of the problems lies in the definition of information technology (IT). Does it represent a subcomponent (e.g., a computer chip), something larger (e.g., a computer or other subsystem), or does it represent the entire weapon system? In many cases, such questions can be resolved by consulting with OSD personnel to define what is required. The process of resolution, in turn, builds up the experience base of program office personnel, who in turn are able to respond faster to the same requirement the next time it arises. These interpretation issues arise even when OSD or the Services provide guidance by way of a policy directive or instruction; the guidance itself is often subject to differences in interpretation.

The experience and training level of program office personnel play a crucial role in how they perceive the statutes and regulations. Highly experienced and trained personnel are able to respond better and faster and may not see a given statute or regulation as burdensome. One of the constraints discussed and identified as burdensome during our interviews with OSD staff was the lack of flexibility in moving money from one appropriation to another, such as from the Procurement appropriation to the RDT&E appropriation, as problems occur in the testing cycle. An experienced program manager would plan and budget to ensure sufficient funds are in the management reserve to address these issues. This does not mean that the program manager would excessively fund an acquisition program in anticipation of a cut, but rather that the management reserve would be set based on historical experience and potential challenges in the program while providing a level of transparency in the program office budget to PEO and OSD staff. This working culture is integral to the experience and training level of the program manager and staff.

The working environment in any program office is a function of how the program manager works with his or her staff and interacts with the PEO and OSD. Human factors, including motivating, encouraging, and rewarding employees, go a long way toward running an efficient program office that has smooth working relations with the PEO and OSD, and may make the program manager and staff feel less burdened. Another important aspect of the working environment is staff size in relation to program activities. A fully staffed program office may be better able to respond to program changes and external events than a smaller staff in a similar program, and may be less burdened by day-to-day regulatory routines or special requests.

All these factors highlight the challenges involved in identifying what is burdensome. Given this contextual background, our interviews suggested the following areas as those currently perceived as burdensome:[1]

- cost reporting requirements
- duplication of information among mandated program status reports
- intellectual property rights
- budget reprogramming and "color of money" issues
- the Competition in Contracting Act (CICA)
- the Truth in Negotiations Act (TINA)
- commercial off-the-shelf (COTS) items
- Operational and Live Fire Testing and Evaluation
- the Clinger-Cohen Act
- small business ventures
- the Buy American Act
- the Core Law and 50-50 Rule
- overarching integrated product teams (OIPTs)
- concepts of jointness and system of systems
- the Joint Tactical Radio System (JTRS) policy on waivers.

---

[1] The first eight items on this list are perennial complaints; these areas have been mentioned repeatedly over the past several decades as potentially burdensome. The remaining items on the list refer to more-recent statutory or regulatory areas.

Each of these areas is associated with one or more statutes or regulations. If there is a statute, there is almost always a set of regulations outlining DoD policy and providing implementation guidance. OSD-level regulations are often reflected in Service-level regulations (in the form of policy and implementation guidance).

In each of these areas, the acquisition officials we interviewed provided one or more anecdotes but no estimates of impacts on cost or time. The anecdotes tended to describe dysfunctional processes and conflicting policies but provided no basis for estimating the consequences on program outcomes or formulating policies to mitigate perceived problems. Interestingly, it appears that in many instances it is not the intent of the statute or regulation that constitutes the problem, but rather how it is implemented. The officials we interviewed recognized that these regulations provide much-needed structure to a complex process and address the legitimate need for oversight and accountability where public funds are involved. But while the numerous anecdotes suggest that the view of statutes and regulations as burdensome at the program office level is widespread, there is scant evidence that persuasively ties a specific statute or regulation to a specific impact on a specific program.

Information obtained from the interviews complemented reviews of past studies and led us to the following general observations:

- Most officials we talked with concurred on the intent of specific policies and said that the approaches adopted to achieve those objectives were the real culprits. Problems experienced during the actual implementation of policies and processes lead to a perception of burden.
- With the objective of executing the program as well as possible, experienced program office personnel spend much of their time "gaming the system" when complying with statutes and regulations; that is, they know how to satisfy the requirement at minimal cost to their program.
- The Services have different cultures and differ in their interpretation and implementation of policies, leading to different costs and different perceptions of burden.
- Compliance with statutes and regulations has become institutionalized in the acquisition process. Most program office personnel consider it routine and part of their jobs.
- Program managers factor the time it takes to comply with statutes and regulations into their program plans. With the exception of nonrecurring efforts related to major milestone decisions, routine compliance in recurring activities is generally planned for and is never on the critical path.

Table 3.1 indicates which organization perceives these statutory and regulatory areas as burdensome based on our interviews. Note that all areas are perceived as burdensome at the program office level, though some are perceived as more burdensome than others, largely as a function of where a program is in its life cycle and the particular issues it is currently dealing with. Table 3.1 also indicates which areas we selected for further analysis; we expand on this at the end of this chapter.

Table 3.1
Statutes and Regulations Perceived as Burdensome

Statute or Regulation	Burden				Included in Category
	OSD	Service	Program Office	Contractor	
Clinger-Cohen Act	X	X	X	X	CCA
Core Law and 50-50 Rule		X	X	X	Core Law and 50-50 Rule
Reprogramming activities			X	X	PPB
Cost reporting			X	X	PSR
Program status reporting			X	X	PSR
OIPT process		X	X	X	PSR
Bayh-Dole Act	X	X	X	X	Technical data
Operational testing activites (DOT&E)		X	X	X	Testing
LFT&E		X	X	X	Testing
CICA			X	X	Not included
TINA			X	X	Not included
COTS			X		Not included
Costs to small business		X	X	X	Not included
Buy American Act	X	X	X	X	Not included
Jointness and system of systems		X	X	X	Not included
JTRS waivers		X	X		Not included

NOTES: CCA = Clinger-Cohen Act. PPB = program planning and budgeting. PSR = program status reporting. DOT&E = Director, Operational Test and Evaluation. LFT&E = live fire test and evaluation.

The following sections summarize the results of our interviews regarding each topic area. For each, we present the perception of the problem and the possible consequences to program offices. We have included suggestions for mitigating the problem when suggested by our interviewees. We have not attempted to validate the perception of problems or assess the effectiveness of any proposed solutions at this time. The discussion of each topic reflects how our interviewees perceive the "burden." Such a perception does not mean that a burden actually exists, or that the purported mechanisms related to that burden are correct. Our research was designed to test the hypothesis that the perceived burden associated with a statute or regulation is in fact burdensome and has consequences to program outcomes. Thus, the following discussion represents hypotheses; statements in them should not be considered fact. Our analysis and our conclusions regarding these hypotheses (perceived burdens) will be documented in a separate report.

Cost Reporting Requirements

OSD requires contractors to provide acquisition cost data on the actual cost expended on a semiannual basis in Contractor Cost Data Reports (CCDRs). Prime contractors have long complained that these reports cost too much and constitute an expense that the program office can avoid. CCDRs require the contractor to report data in a standardized format different from the one they use for internal reporting and management purposes. Such a requirement necessitates dual reporting, which some OUSD(AT&L) staff viewed as a burden. However, the consumers of this data, including the OSD Cost Analysis Improvement Group (CAIG) (under OSD PA&E), independent cost analysis organizations within the Services, and a few program offices, believe that having standardized cost data is critical to enable a comparison across multiple programs, each of which may have a different contractor or be run from a different site. Having data in a standardized format makes it easier to track and analyze current and historical patterns, thereby enabling OSD and the Services to have better oversight across multiple programs. Program offices also tend to benefit from this, since the format is not affected by changes in the contractors' accounting system that may arise due to mergers and splits over the years. A standardized data format makes it easier for the program office to derive reliable estimates on the cost of future acquisition programs. Programs (and their prime contractors) that do not currently report in the standardized format, however, tend to bear a high initial nonrecurring investment to establish a compliant reporting system.

The compliance costs in this category tend to accrue mostly at the contractor level, though program offices spend some time reviewing the data and forwarding it to receiving organizations.

Duplication of Information Among Mandated Program Status Reports

Each program office provides an annual SAR to Congress, quarterly DAES reports to OUSD(AT&L), and quarterly Unit Cost Reports (UCRs) to the Service Acquisition Executive (SAE). Both the SAR and DAES are approved by service acquisition officials (i.e., program executive officers, material command, and/or SAE staff), and the SAR is reviewed and approved at the OSD level before being sent to Congress. The SAR contains information already available in the DAES on a quarterly basis, while the UCR provides unit acquisition cost information that is also included in both the DAES and SAR. According to program office personnel, if the redundancy of information across the three reports could be avoided, it could save the program office valuable time and resources. While each report is designed to provide information to a specific audience, it is conceivable that presenting the common information in the same format across the different reports could minimize the redundancy in effort by the program office staff.

All three reports are generated using the Cost Analysis Reporting System (CARS) database, but CARS users have complained about several aspects of this software, saying that it is difficult to use and unable to tailor input to the characteristics of a particular program, it is difficult to change information already entered, and the database does not allow the user to turn off unnecessary or inappropriate functions. Reformatting the current structure of reports and the CARS database would require a one-time investment, but if the recurring expenses in filling out the reports are a small fraction of the program offices' budgets, such an investment may not be warranted. Tracking these costs would therefore be a useful exercise.

Compliance costs in this category tend to accrue at the program level. Program office personnel generate most of the needed information based on the more detailed databases they use to monitor cost and schedule.

Intellectual Property Rights

The 1980 Patent and Trademark Law Amendments Act, commonly known as the Bayh-Dole Act, requires contractors to provide the government with data rights to intellectual property. The objectives of the Bayh-Dole Act were to encourage maximum participation of small businesses and nonprofit organizations, and, later, large contractors, in federally supported research and development efforts while ensuring that the government retains sufficient rights in relevant inventions to meet possible needs and contingencies. For example, if a company develops a particular military technology and then goes out of business, the government wants to ensure it can continue producing that technology by sharing its intellectual property with another company. Additionally, the military may wish to increase the supply base of a weapon system due to a surge in demand and therefore provide another company with information on how to make that weapon system. Finally, retaining and sharing intellectual property may allow the government to foster competition. Allowing the contractor to own the intellectual property while providing the government a broad license to use it for government purposes has accomplished this. The act also provides a "march-in" right that allows the government to license the technology if the contractor does not use it or commercialize it within a reasonable period of time.

The Freedom of Information Act (FOIA) also applies to intellectual property, which is a disincentive for commercial companies considering entering into a contract with the government, especially in the area of research and development where there is a greater possibility of innovation. The issue here is that while Bayh-Dole protects the intellectual property rights of industry, FOIA may require the public release of that information.

Intellectual property is one element of the broader set of technical data often purchased as part of a government contract. Technical data includes the detailed information necessary for the government to support the system or, in some cases, to introduce a competitive source. Significant program office resources are spent reviewing, approving, and storing contractors' data. Minimizing the technical data requirements would relieve the reporting burden on the contractors, which would translate as lower review costs for the program office.

Budget Reprogramming and "Color of Money" Issues

Congress requires DoD and military program offices to manage their budgets in appropriation categories specific to the type of activity being performed. Roughly speaking, funds are categorized as research, development, testing, and evaluation (RDT&E); procurement; military construction (MILCON); or operations and maintenance (O&M). The Navy has an additional category for ship construction: shipbuilding and construction, Navy (SCN). These appropriation categories have different rules governing how the funds can be expended or transferred between accounts and when the funds expire. For instance, RDT&E funds are used for research and development activities that typically occur prior to production, such as design, technology demonstration, system development, and testing. RDT&E funds are also used in activities related to the modification of a weapon system already in production or when deployed. Procurement funds are used for both low-rate and full-rate production, as well as for certain types of spare parts. O&M funds are used to support a deployed weapon system. MILCON funds are used for building construction, usually on military bases.

Another dimension (or "color") is weapon type and associated appropriation line item. Congress authorizes and appropriates funds by Service and by weapon class (e.g., Air Force tactical aircraft, Navy ships, or Army Aviation, among others). Specific rules govern the transfer of funds among these accounts as well.

In general, these rules are based on threshold values. Congress must approve all transfers among appropriate accounts greater than $10 million in RDT&E or $20 million in procurement at the program office level. Below these thresholds, some discretion is given to the Services, which may also generate rules for managing funds applicable at the PEO or program level.[2]

A program manager is responsible for managing all phases of the program with the constraint of not being able to move money from one appropriation to another. A mature program with activities in multiple life cycle stages (e.g., continuing production, supporting deployed systems, developing modifications for future versions) may be dealing with multiple colors of money simultaneously. The inability to move money from one appropriation to another in response to changing needs within the program can hinder a program manager's effectiveness in getting the most out of available funds. Additionally, complying with the various rules governing each pot of money takes time and resources and affects program efficiency. On the other hand, Congress benefits from these rules by ensuring that the funds are spent in the way it intended.

Competition in Contracting Act

The Competition in Contracting Act (CICA) requires "full and open" competition between prime contractors and subcontractors. CICA was enacted for the purpose of increasing the number of government procurements conducted under these principles, as opposed to contracts that are issued under noncompetitive arrangements such as sole source or set-aside awards. It limits the ability to do "rolling downselect" as part of the acquisition strategy, that is, to make participation in Phase I of a contract a prerequisite for participation in subsequent phases. CICA requires a lengthy Request for Proposal (RFP) effort in which the government solicits proposals from several contractors in an effort to foster full and open competition. These practices are rigid, thereby limiting the discretion of contracting officers. Increasing flexibility in these areas could facilitate a more efficient contracting environment and give managers more options in managing the competitive phases of a program.

---

[2]   The only exception to this rule in the Department of Defense is the Missile Defense Agency, which has one funding line and is allowed to move money across different activities.

The cost of complying with CICA falls mainly on the program office. Program offices are responsible for preparing the RFP and running the source selection process. However, these costs occur only during the competitive phase of a program; a program not currently running a competition would not accrue any CICA compliance costs.

Truth in Negotiations Act

TINA requires the contractor to disclose a significant amount of cost information when negotiating a contract with the government. Such a disclosure necessitates a detailed understanding by DoD cost analysts and contracting officers of the contractor's financial structure, often requiring information to be provided in a Contract Work Breakdown Structure (CWBS) different from the one followed internally by the contractor. The contractor typically spends a significant amount of resources to provide this information and would therefore benefit from relief in reporting requirements in this area. Additionally, the contractor is under pressure to ensure complete disclosure of all information or face a criminal penalty; TINA requires that a corporate officer certify in writing that the costs being reported are correct. As a result, TINA is often cited as an example of a DoD-specific statutory requirement that inhibits the participation of commercial firms that are reluctant to spend the necessary resources to meet this requirement.

Congress significantly revised TINA in 1994 as part of the Federal Acquisition Streamlining Act (FASA), and again as part of the Clinger-Cohen Act provisions included in the National Defense Authorization Act for FY 1996. Some of the revisions include an increased dollar-value threshold, allowing a greater number of lower-price transactions to be negotiated without complying with TINA; an exception for commercial items added to the statutory exceptions in TINA; and a TINA provision that permits agencies to request information other than cost or pricing data, even if cost or pricing data are not required to be submitted.

Most of the costs associated with TINA compliance are born by the contractor, though the program office spends time reviewing the information. Like CICA, TINA mainly applies during a competition or contract award when a contractor provides cost information to the government as part of its proposal.

Commercial Off-the-Shelf Items

Over the past several decades, acquisition reform has been oriented toward making DoD more like a commercial business venture. Besides multiple initiatives to streamline processes, DoD has routinely advocated the procurement of commercial off-the-shelf (COTS) items for integration into weapon systems. These items, developed for a commercially competitive marketplace, are perceived as requiring minimal to no development cost and are therefore economically attractive to DoD.

Commercial products often push the state of the art in technologies critical to many key functions, such as wireless communications and computer chips. As a result, DoD and Congress have pushed for procuring COTS items in major acquisition programs. The challenge lies in ensuring that these COTS items do not need to be modified substantially for integration in complex weapon systems. The greater the modification efforts, the higher the cost and greater the deviation from commercial, market-based economics. National security and increased operational capability requirements prevent DoD weapon systems from incorporating COTS items "as is," thereby calling into question the economic viability of such an alternative. On the other hand, there are opportunities for COTS items to be incorporated into weapon systems without any modifications, making this an issue warranting careful consideration. Time spent identifying potential COTS items for a weapon system would be one example of a cost at the program office level.

Interviews with members of integrated dual-use commercial companies (IDCC)[3] highlighted a case in which DoD issued an RFP for an R&D activity, asking for a product that had already been developed by a commercial firm. The firm offered to sell the existing product to DoD as COTS (it met all DoD requirements) but would not enter into an R&D activity for which there was no need and during which DoD would likely ask for access to proprietary data. DoD refused (only R&D funds were available) and ended up selecting a defense contractor with less expertise.[4] DoD may have had other reasons for choosing the defense contractor. For example, the useful life of a weapon system may span several decades, making technological obsolescence a common problem. DoD policy and cultural biases necessitate gaining access to technical data to ensure that DoD can manage future modifications and updates (see the discussion of intellectual property rights earlier in this section); in a commercial product, that data would be considered proprietary information.

Costs associated with COTS provisions in statutes and regulations are not necessarily concentrated in any one organization. Rather, costs would accrue to different organizations depending largely on the circumstances. A program office purchasing a COTS item for incorporation into a weapon system might accrue costs only if the COTS item needs to be modified. Such costs are not just in terms of time spent (program office staff labor), but would more likely involve additional payments to industry.

Operational and Live Fire Testing and Evaluation

Program offices are responsible for planning and conducting developmental testing (DT) and for supporting operational testing, usually conducted by a Service operational test agency. The DOT&E heads an independent organization within DoD with the authority to assess the operational suitability and effectiveness of a weapon system program, and, based on that assessment, approve entry into full-rate production. The DOT&E may not be involved in the early stages of testing but can set rules and test requirements for the latter stages of testing, requiring the program to demonstrate the effectiveness and operational suitability of the weapon system by passing DOT&E's independently monitored operational testing requirements. The mechanism for this is usually the approval of the Test and Evaluation Master Plan (TEMP) and other operational test planning documents required at milestone decisions. This practice ensures the DOT&E's independence, but the contractor and program office may perceive it as a require-

---

[3]   IDCC is a trade association whose members are commercial firms that have much to offer DoD, but which will not usually contract directly with DoD because of intellectual property, cost accounting, and other DoD-specific policies.

[4]   Examples of products and companies that meet DoD requirements include flat glass (Corning), optical fibers (Corning), specialized film (Kodak), and wireless phones and radios (QUALCOMM).

ment to repeat tests already completed in the DT phase. As a result, many program offices are interested in finding ways to reduce the perceived redundancy in operational testing.

Live fire test and evaluation (LFT&E) occurs at the system, subsystem, and component level. Program offices may perceive such tests as expensive and wasteful, particularly if the system, subsystem, or component is damaged irreparably in the process. The program office therefore invests significant resources to obtain waivers and create alternate testing methods that prove the capabilities of the weapon system while avoiding the costly venture of destroying it. Some program offices have suggested using data from weapon systems exposed to live fire during war operations as a surrogate. Interviewees suggested that efforts to generate test waivers and develop alternate testing methods at the program office level need to be evaluated for effectiveness with the goal of easing implementation and streamlining the process.

The Clinger-Cohen Act

The 1996 Clinger-Cohen Act (CCA), officially known as the Information Technology Management Reform Act, mandated major changes to and established a more stringent process of managing the ways in which federal agencies acquire IT systems. The act stresses the need for joint architectures and interoperability, related training, information security, capital planning, and investment control. This act has created significant confusion over the understanding of the term *IT*. Almost all modern weapon systems include some degree of IT and, depending on the interpretation, are therefore required to be compliant with the Clinger-Cohen Act. Our interviews indicated that one of the main problems is a lack of consistency in how the act is interpreted and implemented, since there are constantly changing rules about which forms to submit and when and how to do so. This inconsistency occurs across Services; between the Services and the Office of the Secretary of Defense, Networks and Information Integration (OSD[NII]); and across commodity commands within a Service. This seems to be a problem of regulatory interpretation, not legislation. There is also an ongoing debate about whether the provisions of the act apply to national security systems and the IT embedded in those systems.

CCA compliance costs accrue mainly at the program office level; most of the reporting is focused on the specific weapon system. Program office staff spend time gathering the information, drafting the reports, and presenting them to the various Service and OSD approving agencies. There is also the potential for a schedule delay to the program if reporting is incomplete at the time of a major milestone decision.

Small Business Ventures

Small businesses attempting to be a part of the DoD acquisition process have to spend significant resources trying to understand the relevant statutes and regulations. This is often burdensome because they have limited resources. Additionally, as mentioned before, the government's interest in intellectual property rights often discourages small businesses from participating in these contracts because they fear losing their competitive edge by divulging proprietary information. Therefore, small businesses typically subcontract from prime contractors that have an understanding of and experience with the DoD acquisition process and the related statutory and regulatory requirements.

The Small Business Innovative Research (SBIR) program was designed to encourage small business participation in military R&D. The SBIR program receives funding from program offices, which contribute a small fraction of their budget in the form of a tax. However, these program offices typically do not see a direct benefit of the tax to their programs. Funds from the SBIR program go toward research activities that are generally not tailor-made to address the technical challenges specific to the program offices. As a result, these program offices typically perceive the SBIR tax as a burden. The compliance cost here is a direct cost rather than time spent by program staff.

The Buy American Act

Congress has been pushing DoD to buy American-made products for its weapon systems acquisition programs. This is particularly difficult in an age of multinational corporations, as U.S.-based companies may have several branches abroad. The push to contract only with U.S. companies reduces the industrial base that can compete for the contracts and may stifle competition and innovation. Some acquisition officials claim that this forces the government to procure less-innovative products at a higher cost.

Compliance costs are diffuse but potentially significant in specific cases. Using a less-innovative or lower-quality product could reduce system performance. Program office time spent finding U.S. producers might be perceived as wasted time.

The Core Law and 50-50 Rule

The Core Law (10 USC 2464) and 50-50 Rule (10 USC 2466) require that public depots perform 50 percent of the DoD-wide maintenance workload. Interviews with some program offices suggested that they spend a significant amount of time ensuring the requirement is met at all levels of the weapon system. This would include trying to get the requirement waived by making a case for the use of a private-sector business so that the work may be contracted to a private organization and working with the public depots to ensure they are technically capable of doing the required maintenance work. Naval Sea Systems Command, on the other hand, interprets the laws differently: Most of its nuclear maintenance work on carriers and submarines is done at public shipyards, thereby meeting the requirement at the command level. These examples highlight the sharp contrast in the implementation process that sometimes exists among the Services.

One program office suggested that smaller programs do not generally deal with these laws because they lack the funding and time to fulfill the requirements. In some cases, the cost of bringing the government depot on par with a commercial depot's capabilities can be high and therefore a deterrent. As new weapon systems are developed, the original equipment manufacturer (OEM) has a technical advantage in terms of maintenance capabilities over the government depots, which have traditionally not been involved in the acquisition process and are therefore not privy to the latest advances. Getting these government depots involved in the System Development and Demonstration (SDD) phase could help prepare them to support the weapon system upon deployment.

Some program offices have suggested a partnership arrangement between the government and commercial depots wherein best business practices could be incorporated. Most program office personnel we spoke to indicated that they spend a significant amount of time developing cases to justify the use of commercial depots and thereby obtain relief from meeting the laws' requirements. Quantification of these efforts would be a first step in trying to assess the burden imposed by these statutes, along with the differences in implementation across the program offices in the Services.

Overarching Integrated Product Teams

In 1995, DoD acquisition policy established Integrated Product and Process Development (IPPD) as the standard approach to structuring program offices. The key element of this policy was the integrated product team (IPT), a multidisciplinary, and often multi-agency, group with specific responsibilities. IPTs are intended to include all relevant stakeholders and can be established at any organizational level within the program, as well as externally in program oversight functions.

The IPT approach is intended to promote better communication within an organization and reduce the time required to build consensus on key issues critical to a program. This is possible, however, only when members of the IPT both participate and have the authority to make decisions for the program. Requiring IPT members to make additional briefings to and obtain approval from senior decisionmakers within their individual organizations greatly reduces the effectiveness of IPTs.

IPTs have proliferated in recent years. There are working-level IPTs (WIPTs), which report to initial integrated product teams (IIPTs), which in turn report to the overarching IPT (OIPT), which then reports to the Defense Acquisition Board (DAB). One program office complained about the OIPT process after having gone through the IIPT process for regulatory, technical, and logistical problems and reaching a consensus. Upon arriving at the OIPT stage, some of the same individuals brought up concerns and questions that were in many cases redundant or irrelevant. The result was five IIPTs and two OIPTs before a Milestone B DAB, and a much more lengthy and involved process than necessary.

Concepts of Jointness and System of Systems

Joint programs across two or more Services reduce redundancy in weapon systems and military capabilities, resulting in some potential savings to DoD and enhancing interoperability. The cost of integrating the Services' acquisition processes and ensuring interoperability falls upon the program offices, however, while the Services and the DoD organization as a whole reap the benefits in savings and performance enhancements. As a result, program offices generally perceive jointness as a burden.

Interoperability challenges also exist when acquiring a suite of systems, with each system performing a unique function and designed to operate together as an emergent system with a distinct function of its own in a system of systems (SoS) mode. Most preconceived SoS efforts to date have been undertaken by individual Services, but a joint SoS is needed to make joint operations more effective. Existing statutes and regulations provide very little support for SoS acquisition. The latest 5000 series documents say nothing about it, although DoD Instruction 5000.2, from May 12, 2003, uses in passing the term "family of systems" in Enclosure 5, "Integrated Test and Evaluation," without explaining what is meant by the term. Similarly,

DoDI 5000.2 says virtually nothing about how to achieve jointness. Although such regulatory silence on these subjects is technically a lack of constraint, regulations in practice are often interpreted as implicitly stating that anything not required is to be ignored. This silence, combined with the difficulty of managing joint programs, may tend to restrict the amount of effort that is devoted to producing a joint SoS.

Joint Tactical Radio System Policy on Waivers

The push by DoD to buy a common JTRS is pursuant to a policy directive issued by OSD, not legislation. The problem is that the radio will not be available until at least 2008, whereas weapon systems that need to incorporate it are being produced currently.[5] One program office we talked to tried to get a waiver from incorporating the JTRS but was turned down. Instead, the office was told to use an interim solution, which itself does not yet exist. Additionally, the program office must obtain annual waivers, even though it has a multiyear production contract. This redundant work requires staffing at the program office that could be otherwise avoided, leading the program office to view the JTRS waiver policy as burdensome.

Burdensome Statutes and Regulations Common to All Programs Interviewed

Despite the variability in the statutes and regulations interviewees identified as burdensome, as well as the relative importance they place on each, there was a great deal of commonality on a more general level. We therefore identified the following statutory and regulatory areas as warranting further examination:

- Clinger-Cohen Act
- Core Law and 50-50 Rule
- program status reporting
- program planning and budgeting
- technical data
- testing

These six statutory and regulatory areas were common among a majority of interviews. We chose these for further analysis because we felt that their familiarity would result in a better response from any given sample of program office personnel. They are not necessarily the most burdensome, but rather reflect areas most program offices need to address and that many in the acquisition community feel may be burdensome.

The issues associated with the Clinger-Cohen Act, the Core Law and 50-50 Rule, and testing are largely the same as those cited in the above discussion. Program planning and budgeting pertains to activities related to reprogramming money from one appropriation to another, as well as other budgetary planning processes. The technical data category includes

---

[5] Since our initial interviews, the JTRS program has experienced technical difficulties that will push back the availability of the radio.

intellectual property rights, but also a broader set of information describing the technical details of a system, produced by the contractor and reviewed by the program office. Program status reporting includes cost reporting, duplicative information, and OIPT process categories, cited in the preceding discussion.

CHAPTER FOUR

Developing and Testing a Tool to Quantify the Impact of Constraints at the Program Office Level

During our interview phase, several program office personnel provided anecdotal information on how much time or effort their respective programs spent on regulatory activities. Officials at all levels consistently communicated the perceived burden of a particular statute or regulation in terms of time spent on compliance activities by program office staff. Unfortunately, anecdotes are susceptible to gross errors in the level of effort recalled, thereby making the quantification process suspect at best. Recording actual hours spent on a specific compliance activity is a relatively more straightforward and accurate approach, assuming the data collection process is well structured.

This chapter discusses how we addressed this challenge, focusing specifically on the six statutory and regulatory areas that emerged from our interviews. We describe our approach to collecting relevant empirical data, the tool we developed to collect that data, and the overarching analytical process in which the tool is embedded. We also discuss the pilot test of the tool and the analysis process we conducted with two program offices.[1]

Collecting Data

Having already answered the question of which statutory and regulatory areas were most frequently cited as burdensome to program offices, we needed to determine what activities program staff performed to comply with these statutes and regulations. We also needed to decide the following: (1) what information we needed about participants, (2) how often we wanted participants to provide input, and (3) what kind of input we wanted participants to provide.

Since most of the program offices we interviewed described the perceived statutory and regulatory burden in terms of the amount of time they spend complying with such mandates, we used "time spent" on specific activities as the basic unit of measure for the research. The activities of interest would need to have a basis in the statutes or regulations of interest; pre-

---

[1] As the project moved into this research phase, we brought on a survey research specialist and a Web designer/ programmer to ensure that the research tool and associated processes would be most likely to produce usable results.

sumably, such compliance activities would not account for 100 percent of an individual staff member's time, except perhaps in certain circumstance (e.g., a staff member spends all of his or her time ensuring that expenditures correspond with the appropriation accounts).

Outlining Key Statutory and Regulatory Activities

Our first step was to review the six statutes and regulations and develop a short list of the most common activities that program office personnel perform to ensure compliance with the goal of incorporating this list into the data collection tool. Table 4.1 shows the specific activities relevant to the six statutory and regulatory areas. This list reflects our understanding of the key

Table 4.1
Activities Listed Under Each Statutory and Regulatory Area

Statutory or Regulatory Area	Compliance Activity
Clinger-Cohen Act	CCA compliance table: develop, update, or revise
	CCA compliance briefing: develop, update, or revise
	CCA compliance confirmation or certification report: develop, update, or revise
	Information assurance strategy: develop, update, or revise
	System or subsystem registry: develop, update, or revise
	Global Information Grid or Joint Technical Architecture compliance
	Other activities related to CCA, Global Information Grid, or Joint Technical Architecture compliance
Core Law and 50-50 Rule	Industrial capabilities section of Acquisition Strategy: develop, update, or revise
	Core/source of repair analysis section of Acquisition Strategy: develop, update, or revise
	Competition analysis section of the Acquisition Strategy: develop, update, or revise
	Annual 50-50 Depot Maintenance Report to Congress: develop, update, or revise
	Other activities related to Core Logistics
Program planning and budgeting	Submit an above-threshold reprogramming action
	Submit a below-threshold reprogramming action
	Descope a portion of the program to pay for a funding shortfall elsewhere
	Conduct what-if exercises to see the effects of changes in funding, schedule, or quantity
	Other activities related to programming and budgeting

Table 4.1—Continued

Statutory or Regulatory Area	Compliance Activity
Program status reporting	Collect data, prepare, or answer questions related to SAR
	Collect data, prepare, or answer questions related to DAES
	Collect data, prepare, or answer questions related to UCR
	Review, analyze, or forward CCDR
	Collect data, prepare, or answer questions related to Acquisition Program Baseline or Alternative System Review
	Collect data, prepare, or answer questions related to Service-specific reports
	Other activities related to cost, schedule, performance, and status reporting
Technical data	Create a data management system for technical data
	Update a data management system for technical data
	Develop CDRLs (DD Form 1498 or equivalent)
	Review technical data deliverables
	Obtain final approval of technical data deliverables
	Store/maintain technical data that has been delivered
	Prepare technical data for use by third party
	Other activities related to the provision of technical data
Testing	Annual Report of DOT&E: develop, update, or revise
	Review requirements document
	TEMP: develop, update, or revise
	Beyond–Low Rate Initial Production report: develop, update, or revise
	Operational Test Plan: develop, update, or revise
	Low-Rate Initial Production/Initial Operation Test and Evaluation Brief: develop, update, or revise
	Full-Rate Production Brief: develop, update, or revise
	Operational Test Readiness Review (OTRR): develop, update, or revise
	Review Live Fire Test plan and strategy
	Obtain Live Fire waiver
	Other activities related to operational and live fire testing

NOTE: Respondents were asked to specify the nature of activities in the "other activities" categories.

compliance activities required by a given statute or regulation.[2] Within each area, we decided to include a category for "other" activities to capture relevant compliance activities that are not explicitly listed.

Prior to fielding the pilot test, preliminary discussions were held at two program offices. During these discussions, both program offices independently argued that most of what their engineering divisions did was review (or make use of) technical data provided by the contractor. Collecting the hours toward technical data–related activities would have therefore captured 100 percent of the effort by personnel working in these divisions. There would have been no way of identifying which specific statutory and/or regulatory activities are burdensome, since they are so deeply embedded in the working culture of the personnel dealing with technical data issues. As a result, we omitted technical data from our list of statutory and regulatory areas prior to fielding the pilot test.[3]

Collecting Participant Information

The goal of this study is to determine the costs to the program office of complying with particular statutes and regulations. Although information about individual participants is generally unnecessary, we realized that certain elements would be important. Assuming participants accurately indicated how much time they spend on the above activities, we could use information on the rank or pay grade of each participant to approximate an hourly rate and thus quantify the total cost expended toward an activity at the program level. This information would also allow us to quantify the total cost of compliance borne by senior staff members within a program office, which may be useful from an analytical standpoint. Additionally, if the program office subcontracts some of the reporting activities relevant to this study to a support contractor, we could use this information in a complementary manner.

We also theorized that a participant's work experience may have a direct link to the time it takes him or her to perform an activity. For instance, a participant who has held the same position for several years may spend less time on these efforts when compared with someone who is new to the job. Likewise, a participant with significant government or military experience may be able to perform certain activities relatively faster. Thus, we decided that asking participants to indicate the number of years of work experience in the job and in government service might enhance our understanding of the level of effort each participant invests toward compliance activities.

Determining the Frequency of Data Collection

Based on our interviews and past studies, our hypothesis was that program office staff and their support contractors spend considerable time and effort complying with statutes and regu-

---

[2]   To develop these lists, the RAND team reviewed the relevant statutes, regulations, policy directives, and implementing guidance in each area.

[3]   This is not to say that compliance activities associated with technical data are not viewed as constraints or as burdensome. Rather, we decided to focus on the five areas in which the variation in the data appeared to be useful to our analysis. If every engineer in a participating program office reported full time against this area, we would learn very little about how differences in time spent are driven by program life cycle, staff experience, and other factors.

lations. Tracking the time they spend on activities required to comply with statutes and regulations is the most direct way of quantifying the level of effort at the program office. Collecting such information as the activities are performed would provide the most accurate data. However, such an endeavor would entail significant effort from the staff, thereby minimizing their likely participation in a voluntary data collection system. The larger the gap between when hours are spent on an activity and when those hours are recorded, however, the less likely it is that those hours will reflect actual time spent.

We realized a compromise was needed, balancing the accuracy of reported data with the need to implement a voluntary reporting system. Since most program offices fill out their timesheets at two-week intervals, we decided that timing the data collection process coincide with the timekeeping periods would make it easier for the program office staff to remember their activities and might encourage their participation. Collecting the data directly from the people doing the work is one of the unique aspects of this research design; most studies on this and related topics rely on data collected by third parties or through indirect observation.

Recording Contextual Information

Quantifying hours alone, such as through a cost-based accounting system, is not sufficient. To understand why an activity is performed in a certain way and why it takes a certain amount of time to perform, we asked participants to provide contextual information concerning their activities and, if appropriate, to comment on why they perceived them to be burdensome. Examples in which information provided by participants would be extremely useful for the analysis included the following:

- time the program office staff spends with OSD personnel clarifying the interpretation of what is meant by IT in the context of a weapon system
- instances in which the same program status information was presented repeatedly (e.g., to several senior members within the Service, OSD, Congress, GAO, and other organizations)
- the conducting of multiple budget drills due to a budget cut request driven by restrictions preventing money from being moved across different appropriations.

We also theorized that it might be helpful to know who was requesting the compliance activities. Efforts made by program office staff to comply with statutes and regulations are typically driven by a number of organizations, including Congress, OUSD(AT&L), PA&E, DOT&E, the PEO within the Services, audit offices and comptrollers within the Services, and the Government Accountability Office, among others. These requests may involve different levels of activity within the program office, depending on who requests the information. For instance, when submitting a DAES, a program office staff member may receive input first from the program manager and then from the PEO in the Service before the report is finally sent to OUSD(AT&L). Such a process would require multiple iterations on the DAES based on feedback from the program manager and the PEO. Additionally, once OUSD(AT&L) receives the DAES, additional questions may be raised, potentially resulting in a repeating of the process at the program manager and PEO levels. Recording who requests the compliance activities, be it one or many organizations, would therefore provide additional insight and a richer understanding of the process of compliance.

By gathering the above information, our approach has the potential to enable us to link the hours spent on an activity to contextual information about the activity, as well as provide some insight into why activities are performed in a certain way. In a sense, it is the first step in linking the anecdotes not only to the actual hours spent at the program office level but also to broader consequences to program outcomes.

Developing a Web-Based Data Collection Tool

To minimize the required effort by program office participants to account for their time, we developed an easy-to-use Web-based data collection tool that would enable the participants to input their activities, time spent, and comments as often as they chose. On their first visit to the site, we asked for basic contact information as well as rank or pay grade and years of experience in the job and in the government. Following registration, and on subsequent visits to the site, participants could input individual time spent on specific statutory and regulatory activities for a biweekly reporting period, document who requested the activities, and provide comments related to the hours expended. The Web site's database collects qualitative and quantitative information related to activities in five statutory and regulatory areas:

1. Clinger-Cohen Act
2. Core Law and 50-50 Rule
3. program status reporting
4. program planning and budgeting
5. testing.

We also designed the site to include space where participants could provide information on any other statutory or regulatory area or activity they considered burdensome.

Participants could enter the time spent on a specific activity along with comments related to that activity, which provide the qualitative information. These comments are a crucial step toward the quantification of anecdotes at the program office level. Additionally, participants can indicate which individual or organization requested the activity. For example, a participant could select "program status reporting"; then note the number of hours spent on the DAES; indicate that the effort was directed by OSD; and comment on whether it was an effort related to revision, collecting information, or clarification with OSD personnel. For each activity, the participant can mark one or more check boxes to indicate which organizations requested the effort. For example, OSD may request a report, but the program manager and PEO may request to be briefed on the report prior to its submission to OSD. In this case, the activity is performed for all three organizations.

On the final page of the Web site's input form, two general text boxes capture any additional information a participant might want to convey. One text box asks if anything unusual happened during the reporting period. The second asks if there is anything else RAND should know about program activities and events affecting the program.

The Web site also includes administrative tools to help manage participation. These include simple forms that let participants recommend other program office personnel for participation in the study or tell us about vacations and temporary duty (TDY) periods so we can adjust the data accordingly.

The Overarching Analytical Process

To gain the participation of programs and individuals within those programs, we extended a broad confidentiality assurance to study participants. In particular, knowledge of the identity of the programs supplying information would be limited to the study team. We also agreed to not associate specific information with specific individuals. Thus, we designed the data collection and analysis process to keep private the identities of the participants, which we hoped would encourage more candid responses.

We envisioned RAND researchers assigned to follow specific programs, with real-time follow-up of the information provided by the participants via the Web-based data collection protocol. Of special interest would be the qualitative information users provided in the free-response text boxes. Thus, information of special interest—complaints about specific regulations or procedures, descriptions of events affecting the program, and so on—could be addressed quickly by contacting the individual users who provided the information.

Aside from asking selected program office staff to enter their activities and hours, our overall research approach includes follow-up interviews with program office staff on specific compliance activities that may lead to such program outcomes as cost and schedule overruns. These interviews should provide a richer understanding of the true cost of compliance. Following up on specific comments provided by the program office staff concerning specific compliance hours should provide better perspective on program outcomes related to the particular task(s). For example, a program office may be spending a significant number of hours on reprogramming actions related to color of money issues. Following up on this activity through interviews with the staff may shed light on how the reprogramming actions actually affect the program schedule and cost. As a result, the total cost of compliance would include not only the time program office staff spend on the activity but also the impact the activity has on program costs via-à-vis delays in meeting target dates for specific deliverables.

The overall research approach holds great promise but is heavily dependent on the willingness of the program office management and staff to participate, as each participant will need to enter his or her individual time spent on statutory or regulatory activities. Nevertheless, recording these hours over a one-year period should capture the ebb and flow of activities over the course of an annual cycle at the program office. Additionally, we expect that documenting the program consequences whenever possible will provide the true cost of compliance for certain specific activities.

Overall, the validity of our approach rests on several key assumptions:

- Programs will agree to participate.
- Programs can identify which staff need to register.
- Staff will actually register.
- Participants will be able to divide their time into discrete categories (activities).
- Participants will provide honest input.
- Participants will continue to provide input over a 12-month period.

We recognized that asking individuals to participate over a 12-month period would require a plan to keep them engaged for that long. Thus, we planned for periodic real-time email reminders to individuals who haven't yet provided input for a given period. We also plan to hold quarterly feedback briefings with each participating program office. These sessions will allow us to present to each program the data they have provided, our interpretation of that data, and ask for help in refining that interpretation.

Pilot Phase Testing of the Web-Based Tool

Two program offices pilot tested the Web-based data collection tool to ensure that we correctly captured the key compliance activities and that the Web site was as user-friendly as possible. The E-2C and Apache Attack Helicopter program offices volunteered to participate for two reporting periods (four weeks total) with the understanding that, if the test was successful, they would participate in the full 12-month data collection period. Both programs, as well as their Program Executive Officers, participated in our earlier round of interviews.

After completing the pilot test, participants from both program offices indicated that the Web site was easy to use. Upon reviewing their inputs, however, we realized that since program office personnel typically work across multiple activities within an area, they appeared to have a difficult time keeping track of the total time spent toward a specific activity. In many cases, participants entered hours under "other activities" within an area or under "other statutes or regulations," and we needed to reassign the hours to the appropriate activity or area. The participants recognized that this was part of an initial learning process and indicated that they thought it would be easier to enter their hours once they became more familiar with the site's organization. While we did see some improvement during the pilot test in a given participant's ability to categorize his or her activities, we also determined that additional training of participating program offices was needed.

Results from the pilot test helped validate the list of compliance activities under each statutory and regulatory area. Feedback from these two program offices resulted in significant changes, including modifications to the wording of the activity descriptions and to the activity lists themselves. This improved our confidence that the activity lists captured the key compliance requirements in each area.

The pilot test experience also indicated that somewhat more participants within a program office would need to enroll than we had anticipated. The focus on five specific statutory and regulatory areas was meant in part to limit participation; while these five areas cover important functions, they do not constitute all that a program office does. Nevertheless, the pilot test indicated that program offices would need to spend some time up front identifying exactly who should enroll in the study, and that in order to capture the full level of effort, relatively more participants in each program would be necessary. In general, however, indications were that the necessary number of participants would be about one-third or less of the total program office staff.

Overall, the pilot phase testing was considered a success, with the understanding that the research team would need to put forth additional effort to orient new participants on how to allocate their hours toward specific activities. No hardware or software problems arose during the pilot phase implementation. Program office management and staff demonstrated a willingness and ability to participate. With OUSD(AT&L) approval, the next step was to implement this data collection tool across eight programs, including the two participating pilot phase program programs.

This study is motivated by the perception that a significant portion of program office staff spend the majority of their time complying with statutes and regulations that are perceived as burdensome. From a substantive point of view, the pilot test results seemed to suggest several preliminary observations worth examining during the subsequent full data collection and analysis phase. These include:

- Less than one-quarter of total program office staff work in one or more of the five focus areas.
- Most individuals reported less than full-time work across these five statutory and regulatory areas. A few individuals did report such full-time work, and they tended to be non-senior (e.g., a rank or pay grade lower than 05/GS-14/15 equivalent).
- In total, the hours reported represent about 25 percent of the total time available to participating individuals. That is, on average, the participating individuals spend about 25 percent of their available time on compliance activities associated with the five statutory and regulatory areas.

If these results hold true during the full 12-month data collection period, this would seem to indicate results slightly at variance with our expectations.

CHAPTER FIVE

Research Summary and Next Steps

Research Summary

The overall objective of our research was to identify commonly perceived burdensome statutes and regulations at the program office level within the DoD organization, quantify the level of burden and adverse consequences to program outcomes, and help DoD develop reforms to lessen the burden of compliance. Through application of a unique methodology, we hope to provide empirical evidence linking specific provisions in statutes and regulations with specific consequences at the program level. A complete analysis of this issue would include an assessment of compliance costs and consequences at the contractor, program office, PEO, commodity command, Service functional staff, and OSD functional staff levels. A complete analysis would also include an assessment of the benefits of such compliance activities and their products at all of the above organizational levels, as well as at the congressional level. We chose to focus our research on costs and consequences at the program office level because that is where many of the anecdotes about burden and adverse consequences of compliance originate. To our knowledge, this is the first empirical, systematic study of the impacts of regulations on defense acquisition programs. It is intended to be the first step toward providing greater insight into such impacts, as well as a firmer basis for developing acquisition policy

Our review of past research and our discussions with program office, Service, OSD, and industry officials led to the following general observations:

- The costs and benefits of statutes and regulations are incurred at different levels within the DoD organization. For example, program offices may perceive compliance-related activities as a burden because they pay for them, whereas it is offices within OSD that benefit from the activities.
- Experienced staff members within the program offices are often better trained and better prepared to deal with statutes and regulations. Typically, they anticipate the compliance activities in advance and consider it part of their jobs. This working culture suggests how institutionalized statutes and regulations have become. Additionally, they typically spend most of their time "gaming the system" when complying with statutes and regulations.
- Excluding major milestones, routine compliance activities are never on the critical path and therefore do not impact negatively on the program in terms of cost and schedule.

- Interpretation and subsequent implementation of a newer statute or regulation imposes a significant burden at the program office level. For example, with the Clinger-Cohen Act, significant confusion exists around the understanding of information technology as it applies to weapon systems.
- Services differ in how they interpret and ultimately comply with statutes and regulations. For example, with regard to the Core Law and 50-50 Rule, the Army interprets and complies with the requirement at the weapon system or even subsystem level, while the Naval Sea Systems Command attempts to meet the requirement at the command level.

Over the course of many interviews, five areas mentioned were frequently perceived as burdensome at the program office level. We used these common areas in our final data collection protocol:

1. Clinger-Cohen Act
2. Core Law and 50-50 Rule
3. program planning and budgeting
4. program status reporting
5. testing.

We developed a Web-based data collection tool with the objective of quantifying the efforts toward compliance in these areas (we later omitted technical data at the suggestion of the pilot test participants). The Web site and database allow participants to enter on a biweekly basis actual hours spent on compliance at the individual level within a program office.

Two program offices, E-2C and Apache, volunteered to participate in the pilot phase testing of the Web-based tool over two reporting periods (four weeks total). This was an overall success; participants found the Web site to be quite user-friendly, the compliance activities lists were validated, and participants found that with some repetition, they would be able to accurately divide their time among the categories. We successfully collected quantitative and qualitative data over the four-week period without any software or hardware problems. We found, however, that we need to put forward a significant initial effort to train new participants on how to allocate their hours among specific activities listed in the five different areas, given the fact that program office staff typically work on multiple activities during a given day and over a two-week reporting period.

Next Steps

The next step was to implement this data collection tool across eight volunteering program offices, including the two that volunteered in the pilot phase. We will include programs with a broad range of characteristics, including a variety of life cycle stages (e.g., in production, working toward a major milestone decision, and so on), at least one program representing each Service, and several different weapon system types. Programs will be chosen based on discussions with our OUSD(AT&L) sponsor, the PEOs, and, of course, the program managers.

Data will be collected over a 12-month period in an effort to capture monthly, quarterly, and annually recurring activities. In addition to the challenge of recruiting six additional program offices,[1] getting all programs to start the 12-month data collection process at the same time is anticipated to be difficult. This suggests the possibility of implementing a "rolling start" approach wherein we would stagger the initial participation date of the program offices based on their availability, with the understanding that we would collect qualitative and quantitative information over a 12-month period from each program's start date.

The research plan includes holding quarterly meetings with the program offices to collect contextual information on the major challenges facing the program and how they relate to the five compliance areas. During these meetings, follow-up discussions will be conducted on specific activities that may have a direct impact on program outcomes, for example, in the form of cost and schedule delays. This should provide a more complete understanding of the true cost of compliance in certain specific areas and related activities. Participants will be encouraged to provide qualitative comments on areas they consider burdensome and to suggest ways to improve the status quo. This information will be analyzed and consolidated in an effort to find subsequent relief measures by working with OSD personnel on those statutes and regulations for which our quantitative and qualitative data indicate a significant level of burden over the 12-month data collection period.

Our goal is to identify specific instances in which compliance with acquisition-related legislation or regulations has led to an identifiable penalty, such as time lost, additional cost incurred, loss of system capability, additional demands on critical staff, or some other imposition on the program office. If no effects can be proven through the documentation process, we will identify that as well. If significant effects are found, we will develop alternative concepts for mitigating those constraints.

---

[1] A participating program would need to be convinced that its participation would, first, do no harm, and second, potentially benefit it and other programs in the future through a reduction in compliance burden.

User Manual for the Web-Based Tool

A version of this user manual was provided in both hard copy and electronic form to the individuals from each program participating in the pilot study.

Dear Participant:

Welcome to RAND's Empirical Analysis of the Statutory and Regulatory Environment. This research is sponsored by Mr. Michael Wynne, Acting Under Secretary of Defense (Acquisition, Technology, and Logistics). The objective of our study is to empirically link specific statutes and regulations to specific impacts on particular programs.

You have been identified by your program manager as someone who spends time complying with the particular statutes or regulations of interest in this study. We are asking you to access a Web form every two weeks for the next 52 weeks to log hours worked on activities related to specified statutes or regulations. It takes approximately 10 minutes to complete this form.

This exercise is intended to capture the time taken by program personnel (and, ultimately, the cost to the program) to comply with (or respond to) selected statutes and regulations governing the defense acquisition process. This Web-based data collection form is an important element of our research approach.

We will use the information you provide for research purposes only. Results will be reported in summary fashion; no individuals will be identified in the reports.

This manual provides an introduction to the Web form. You should keep this as a reference during the study. Please contact Melissa Bradley at (703) 413-1100, ext. 5433, if you have any comments, questions, or concerns. You may also contact us at sarc-admin@rand.org.

Thank you for assisting with this important research.

Sincerely,

Irv Blickstein   Jeff Drezner
Co–Principal Investigator   Co–Principal Investigator

Background

It is widely believed that DoD program managers operate under a series of legal or regulatory constraints that stifle innovation, impair productivity, and result in increased costs and time. Every program manager and acquisition executive has experienced frustration in dealing with the regulatory environment imposed on weapons acquisition. Prior research, by RAND and others, has assembled many anecdotes but no reliable estimates of impacts on cost or time. Data to support these claims are simply not collected during the course of routine program execution.

Working with the leadership in OUSD(AT&L) and other appropriate OSD, Service, and program offices, the RAND National Defense Research Institute (NDRI) has identified statutes or regulations of particular interest and developed a data collection protocol to generate the data needed to assess the effects of legal or regulatory constraints on program outcomes. The goal is to document comprehensively any impacts on program outcomes.

This research is being carried out over a period of two years and is divided into three interrelated phases:

Phase 1: Research design. During Phase 1, NDRI researchers reviewed and assessed existing studies on legislative or regulatory constraints on acquisition processes, visited multiple program offices to identify the most burdensome statutes or regulations, and designed the overall research approach and the data collection protocol.

Phase 2: Data collection. This phase implements a Web-based data collection protocol and conducts the supporting analyses needed to properly interpret the data collected in the protocol. The task is envisioned to take approximately 16 months to complete, including the four-week pilot test of the data collection protocol that has already concluded. NDRI will work closely with eight participating program offices to ensure that the data collection is accurate and is only minimally disruptive to the primary mission of the program.

Phase 3: Analysis and implementation. After the data collection period, NDRI will perform a comprehensive analysis of the data collected in Phase 2 and work with OSD to develop alternatives to mitigate the most burdensome statutes and regulations quantified in Phase 2.

Because of the need for primary data collection, this research will require the support of OSD and Service acquisition leadership, and the full participation of the programs implementing the data protocol.

We are currently in the data collection phase of the research.

Study Methodology

Sample

RAND and the project sponsor will identify programs of interest. Program managers will be asked to identify individuals working in their programs who spend time complying with specific statutes or regulations. These program office personnel, including the program managers themselves, will be recruited as participants.

During the study, participants may identify colleagues who also spend time complying with the particular statutes or regulations of interest in this study. These individuals may also be enrolled as study participants.

Timeline

The field period for the data collection activity is 52 weeks. The data collection officially begins on Monday, June 28, 2004. Each program will be participating for 52 weeks (26 two-week study periods). However, program offices may begin their participation on different dates, and participants may join the study after it is already in progress for a given program office (if they are recommended by a colleague, for example). Therefore, your initial login may not be on Monday, June 28, 2004, but at a later date. Our records will keep track of each program office's start and end dates and participants will be notified when their participation in the study has concluded.

Participants will initially register with the study by logging into the study Web site (http://web2.rand.org/sarc/login.asp or http://www.rand.org/sarc/login.asp) and entering a general login (rand) and password (pass). Participants will then be asked to enter their contact information and choose a personal login and password. Once enrolled, participants will be able to access the Web form at any time during the field period.

Entry Periods

For the purposes of this study, the timeline is divided into entry periods. Each entry period is two weeks in length, beginning on a Monday and closing on the Sunday of the second week. Participants will report cumulative time spent on the activities of interest during each two-week entry period.

Participants are asked to access the study Web form at least once during each two-week entry period to log hours worked on activities related to specific statutes or regulations. Participants will be required to "close out" each entry period by the last Sunday of that period. An entry period must be closed out before data for the next entry period can be entered.

Reminders

If the entry period is not closed out, the participant will receive an email prompt the following Monday (and, if necessary, on Wednesday) reminding them to do so. If the period has still not been closed out by the following Thursday, RAND project personnel will attempt to contact the participant directly, or may enlist the assistance of the program manager or his or her designates to determine why a participant has not closed out a period. The Web site includes a form on which users can report in advance any temporary duty (TDY), vacation, or other leaves of absence that would make participation difficult.

Confidentiality

We will use the information participants provide for research purposes only. RAND will not share the specific information provided by participants. Results will be reported in summary fashion; no individuals will be identified in the reports.

RAND Points of Contact

Study Web site: http://web2.rand.org/sarc/login.asp or http://www.rand.org/sarc/login.asp

If you have any technical difficulties, please email sarc-admin@rand.org.

If you have any comments, questions, or concerns about the study you may send us an email or call (703) 413-1100 ext. 5433.

Data Entry Guidelines

The system has been designed so that participants need enter data only once, at the end of each entry period. However, the system will allow the user to access the form multiple times during an entry period. Within a given period, each time a user accesses the Web site, prior data entries for that period will be shown and can be modified.

The following are important data entry guidelines:

- Hours for the entry period should be cumulative. If you initially enter time spent on a specific activity during the first part of the entry period, and then work additional hours on that activity during the second part of the period, you will need to enter the *total* time spent to date in the hours box. For example, If you spent five hours during the first week of the entry period creating a CCA compliance table, then an additional three hours in week two of the entry period updating the table, the total time logged for that activity should be eight hours.

- Enter only positive integers in the hours and minutes fields; fractions and text are not valid entries in these fields.

- Once you have entered information on the activity page and continued to the list of statutes and regulations, if you need to go back and change data, you should select the link rather than use your browser's back button.

- Comment boxes are available on both the activity pages and on the Review Entries page. Please use these comment boxes to note other information about the activity, general comments about your activities, as well as anything unusual about your activity during the entry period. These text boxes are intended to provide us with additional information that may be important to understanding the specific activity information you provide. We strongly encourage their use.

Overview of the Web Form

To access the study Web site, go to either of the following pages: http://web2.rand.org/sarc/login.asp or http://www.rand.org/sarc/login.asp.

This first page provides background information on the study and prompts for a login and password. The initial login is **rand** and the password is **pass**; you will need to create your own personal login and password during your first visit to the Web site. On subsequent visits, you should access the Web site by entering your personal login and password.

If you have forgotten you login and password, select **Email me my password** from the login page. You will be asked to provide your email address. Type in your full email address and select the **Email me my password** button at the bottom of the screen. You will receive an email message with your login name and password within a few minutes.

Contact Information

On your initial visit to the Web site, you will be asked to provide your contact and job-related information and to select a personal login name and password so that we may enter you into the system.

Contact Information Screen

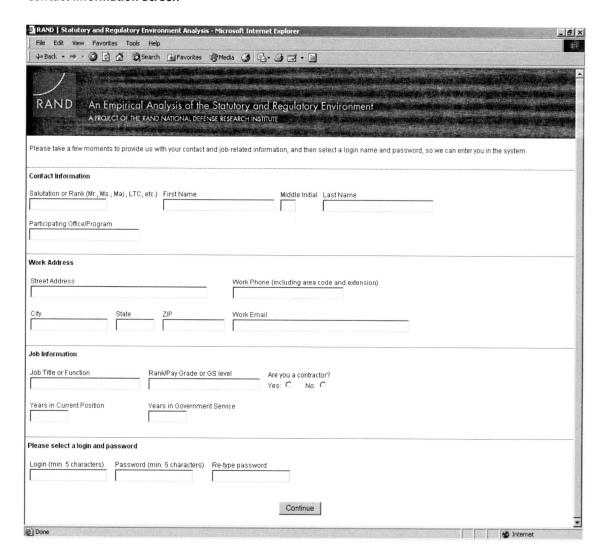

Please provide complete information in each field. The system will prompt you if required fields are not completed.

Your login and password must be a minimum of five characters. Logins and passwords are *not* case sensitive. You may select any combination of letters, numbers, or characters, other than spaces, for your login and password.

If your initial login is after the first entry period (June 28, 2004, to July 11, 2004), you will have the option of entering data for the period just prior to your login period. If, during the two-week period prior to your beginning the study, you spent time on statutory or regulatory activities, please select **Continue and enter data for the previous period** to save your contact information and enter data for the previous study period.

If you did not spend any time on statutory or regulatory activities during the previous period, select **Continue and enter data for this period** to save your contact information and enter data only for the current study period.

Welcome/Welcome-Back Page

During your initial login, after your contact information has been entered and login chosen, you will enter the Welcome page; when you log in to the Web form on a return visit, you will enter the Welcome-Back page. From this page, you can select the statutes and regulations for which you would like to submit data. On the Welcome-Back page, you will also find links to pages for updating personal information, notifying the project about vacations or TDY, discontinuing participation, or notifying the project of colleagues who should be enrolled in the study.

On the banner of these pages, you can note the current date and current period date range, and access the online help pages (see Appendix B of this user manual for a description of the online help options). The period date range indicates the period for which data should be entered.

To update information relevant to your participation in the study from this screen, select from the bottom of the Welcome-Back page the appropriate link, as indicated below.

Welcome Page

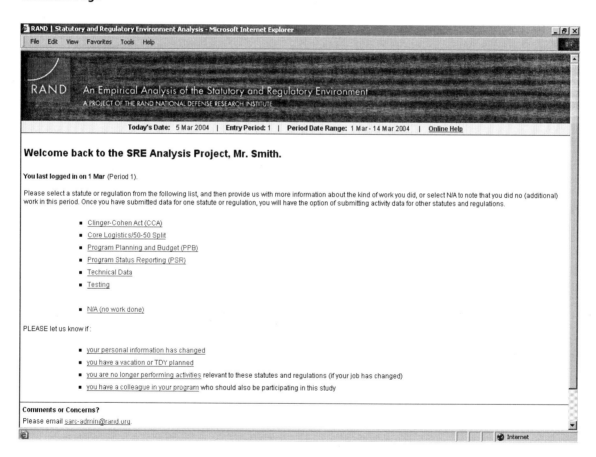

Updating Personal Information

You should select **your personal information has changed** when you need to update information in your profile. This includes changes in job function or title, work phone number, and email address.

To update personal data, enter the new information in the appropriate fields of the Web form. Select the **Update Contact Information** button at the bottom of the screen to save the changes. Data can be updated or changed during any session.

Update Contact Information

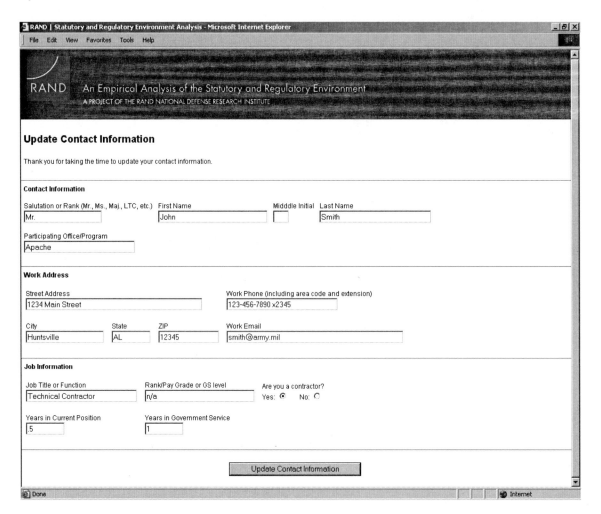

Vacations/TDY

If you will not be available for a period of time due to extended travel or TDY, this can be reported by selecting the **you have a vacation or TDY planned** link. Complete this form to inform the project team of planned absences and, when possible, to identify a temporary replacement to provide information about the program in your absence. If you will be doing statutory or regulatory activities while on TDY but will not have access to the Internet, you can enter that information after you return. Please email sarc-admin@rand.org, and we will provide you with other ways to record your activities during your TDY.

Select the **Submit Vacation/TDY Notification** button at the bottom of the screen to save this data.

Notification of Vacation or TDY

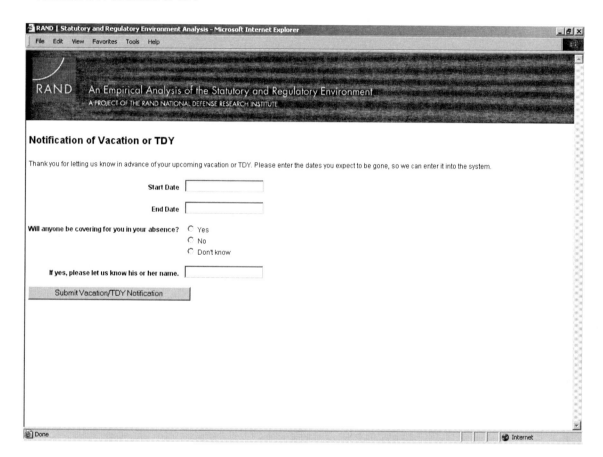

Discontinuing Participation

You should notify the project as soon as possible if your position changes or if you are no longer performing activities related to the statutes and regulations of interest to this project. Select **you are no longer performing activities** and indicate your departure date (if known) so we can update the database and cancel your participation. In addition, if you know of a colleague who is taking over your assignments and should therefore be added to the project, please provide that person's name so that we may contact him or her directly.

Select the **Submit Notification** button at the bottom of the screen to submit the notification.

Discontinuing Participation

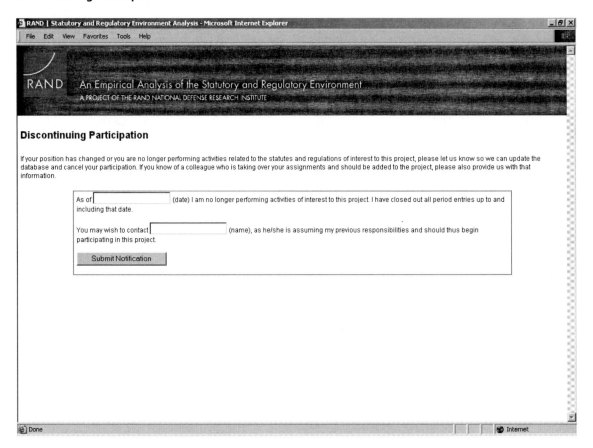

Recommend a Colleague

If you know of a colleague who performs activities of interest to this project, you can submit that person's name and contact information to the study. Please select **you have a colleague in your program** and provide that person's contact information on the Web form. We will contact that person to determine his or her eligibility for the study.

Select the **Submit Notification** button at the bottom of the screen to send this information to the study.

Recommend a Colleague

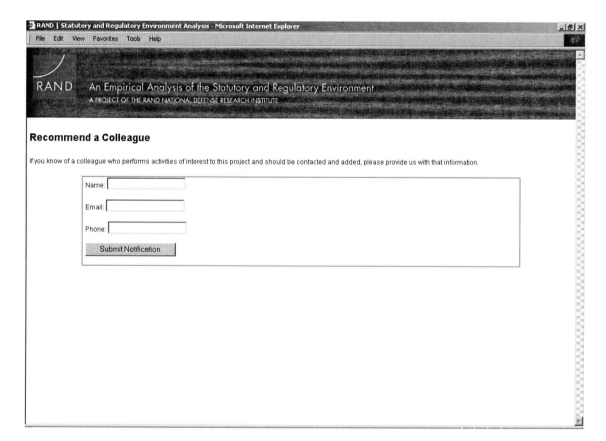

Activity Pages

To provide the study with information about the time spent on activities related to specific statutes or regulations, select the statute or regulation from the list on the Welcome-Back page. When you select a statute or regulation on the Welcome-Back page, related activities will appear on a new screen.

We have generated the list of specific activities on each activities page based on our review of the relevant statutes, regulations, and policies. All activity pages include an "other activity" section to capture time spent on activities that are related to the particular statute or regulation but not otherwise listed.

You may note the specific activities you have performed during the entry period by checking the appropriate boxes. Also note the total time spent to date (within the entry period) on that activity and the entity or person for whom the work was completed. You may also note any other information about the activity in the **Other Information/Comments** box. Be sure to enter data for all activities performed during the entry period.

The **Other Information/Comments** box is an important part of the Web form and we strongly encourage its use. This space is for any additional information that you feel is important to understanding the time you spent. For example, if you spent two days on a task that in other periods has only taken ten minutes, you might want to elaborate on the reason for the difference.

Sample Clinger-Cohen Act (CCA) Activities Page

RAND | Statutory and Regulatory Environment Analysis - Microsoft Internet Explorer

File   Edit   View   Favorites   Tools   Help

RAND   An Empirical Analysis of the Statutory and Regulatory Environment
A PROJECT OF THE RAND NATIONAL DEFENSE RESEARCH INSTITUTE

Today's Date: 5 Mar 2004 | **Entry Period:** 1 | **Period Date Range:** 1 Mar - 14 Mar 2004 | Online Help

Clinger-Cohen Act (CCA) Activities - Period 1

For a brief description of Clinger-Cohen Act (CCA)-related activities and definitions of terms, go to the Online Help pages.

From the following list, select as many Clinger-Cohen Act (CCA)-related activities as you performed in Period 1 to date (1 Mar - 14 Mar 2004). Let us know for whom you performed each activity (select all that apply) and how much time you spent on it. If you performed activities not otherwise listed, please use the Other Activities box to provide a complete description of each activity and who requested it, and indicate the time you spent on it. Then click Continue at the bottom of the page.

- CCA compliance table -- develop, update, or revise
- CCA compliance briefing -- develop, update, or revise
- CCA compliance confirmation or certification report -- develop, update, or revise
- Information Assurance (IA) strategy -- develop, update, or revise
- System or subsystem registry -- develop, update, or revise
- Collect, analyze, or present information related to GIG or JTA compliance
- Other activities related to CCA, GIG, or JTA compliance (please specify)

Activity	Time Spent	For Whom	Other Information / Comments
☐ CCA compliance table -- develop, update, or revise [Definition]	Hours: Minutes:	☐ OSD ☐ Service ☐ DoD CIO / C3I ☐ Service CIO / C3I ☐ PEO / PM ☐ Unknown ☐ Other (please specify)	
☐ CCA compliance briefing -- develop, update, or revise [Definition]	Hours: Minutes:	☐ OSD ☐ Service ☐ DoD CIO / C3I ☐ Service CIO / C3I ☐ PEO / PM ☐ Unknown ☐ Other (please specify)	
☐ CCA compliance confirmation or certification report -- develop, update, or revise [Definition]	Hours: Minutes:	☐ OSD ☐ Service ☐ DoD CIO / C3I ☐ Service CIO / C3I ☐ PEO / PM ☐ Unknown ☐ Other (please specify)	
☐ Information Assurance (IA) strategy -- develop, update, or revise [Definition]	Hours: Minutes:	☐ OSD ☐ Service ☐ DoD CIO / C3I ☐ Service CIO / C3I ☐ PEO / PM ☐ Unknown ☐ Other (please specify)	
☐ System or subsystem registry -- develop, update, or revise [Definition]	Hours: Minutes:	☐ OSD ☐ Service ☐ DoD CIO / C3I ☐ Service CIO / C3I ☐ PEO / PM ☐ Unknown ☐ Other (please specify)	
☐ Collect, analyze, or present information related to GIG or JTA compliance [Definition]	Hours: Minutes:	☐ OSD ☐ Service ☐ DoD CIO / C3I ☐ Service CIO / C3I ☐ PEO / PM ☐ Unknown ☐ Other (please specify)	
☐ Other activities related to CCA, GIG, or JTA compliance (please specify) [Definition]	Hours: Minutes:	☐ OSD ☐ Service ☐ DoD CIO / C3I ☐ Service CIO / C3I ☐ PEO / PM ☐ Unknown ☐ Other (please specify)	

[Continue]

Done   Internet

Select the **Continue** button at the bottom of the screen to submit the data.

Once you have submitted data for one statute or regulation, you have the option of submitting activity data for other statutes and regulations. Click on the appropriate link and repeat the process. All activity pages are structured in the same way.

Below, we provide a brief description of each statute or regulation included on the list.

1. Clinger-Cohen Act (CCA)

Clinger-Cohen Act–related activities refer to provisions in the Information Technology Management Reform Act of 1996 (ITMRA, Division E of the fiscal year [FY] 1996 National Defense Authorization Act) that set rules (provisions) for the management of information systems and technology in federal agencies, including DoD. In general, most weapon systems meet the definition of a National Security System contained in the act, and so must comply with the law's provisions, as implemented through DoD policy (DoD Instruction 5000.2). Also included are the provisions in PL 105-261, Subtitle D (National Defense Authorization Act of 1999), which sets additional responsibilities for the chief information officer (CIO). For our purposes, we are interested in any and all activities undertaken at the program level to comply with CCA or related DoD policy and implementation guidance associated with managing information technology and resources, including the Global Information Grid (GIG) and the Joint Technical Architecture (JTA). This includes activities related to the Information Technology Acquisition Board.

2. Core Logistics/50-50 Split

The Core logistics capability requirement and the 50-50 depot maintenance requirement are laid out in Title 10 of the U.S. Code, Sections 2464 and 2466. We are interested in any activities undertaken at the program level to collect, monitor, or report data or other information regarding the maintenance needs of your weapon system. Many of these activities support logistics or maintenance sections of the program's Acquisition Strategy Report (ASR), or are required to support decisions regarding the support plan for a system. For example, time spent reallocating funding in order to meet the 50-50 criteria should be reported. On the other hand, time spent dealing with reprogramming or new budgeting actions, even when they involve the funding for depot maintenance, should be reported on the Program Planning and Budgeting page.

3. Program Planning and Budget (PPB)

The Programming and Budgeting processes within the Department of Defense are both complex and time consuming. Because a Service or agency balances its total resource plan when submitting either a Program Objectives Memorandum (POM) or a budget, priorities for resources are not always clear to those in the chain of command. This set of activities, in response to many in the Acquisition Process, is intended to capture the time taken by program personnel professionals (and, hence, the cost incurred by the program) to respond to the specific requests for program or budget information.

4. Program Status Reporting

This section addresses key reporting requirements provided on a regular or one-time basis by the program office to a variety of sponsors, including OSD(AT&L), Congress, and Services, among others. We have included the SAR, DAES, UCR, CCDR, Acquisition Program Baseline (APB), and ASR in this section. There are also Service-specific monthly status reports or reports responding to inquiries on current program cost, schedule, and performance issues from a variety of sponsors. These could be included under the "other activities relating to cost, schedule, performance, and status reporting" category.

5. Testing

The Testing page is intended to capture the effort of the program office staff in managing test efforts, planning tests, and utilizing test results for key decisionmakers involved in leading major defense acquisition programs. This effort is primarily interested in capturing those efforts directly rooted in statute; thus, only those major defense acquisition programs receiving oversight (as listed on the DOT&E oversight list) should be included in the data collection effort. If testing-related events, listed on the testing activities page, cause a change in schedule or budget, please report the level of effort spent reallocating resources on the Program Planning and Budget (PPB) activities page. Since testing and system requirements are so interrelated, we ask you to capture the time spent in requirements review and updating requirement documents (Initial Capabilities Document [ICD], Capability Development Document [CDD], Capability Production Document [CPD]) related to testing (e.g., requirement modifications due to test-identified shortfalls, clarification of vague or untestable requirements, etc.). Please use the Other Activities category to capture activities not otherwise indicated, such as significant test-related analysis or related work in preparation for Design Readiness Reviews.

6. Other Statutes or Regulations

We have included this page as a way for participants to identify and describe any other statute or regulation that is perceived as particularly important or time-consuming for the program office. Examples include Forcign Military Sales, contracting policy, and personnel management. This will allow the study team to gain insight into some of the other statutes and regulations affecting DoD program offices, thus identifying areas that may require the attention of OSD policymakers in addition to the five areas that are the primary focus of this research.

Logging Out

Once you have completed your entries for each relevant statute or regulation, select **review your entries** from the menu. This will take you to the Review Entries page. The data you have entered for the entire period date range will be displayed. You can modify entries for any statute or regulation by choosing the link next to that statute's name, or you may add activities from other statues and regulations by choosing the **Return to List of Statutes and Regulations** link at the top of the page. You may also completely delete the data for any given activity by choosing the **delete** button next to the hours for that activity.

Review Entries Page

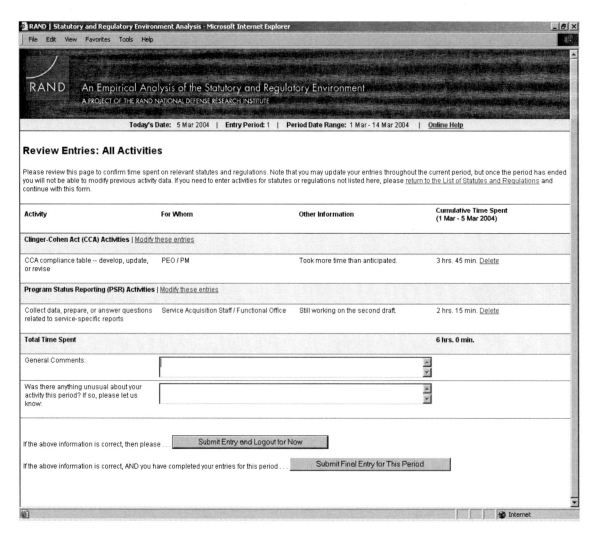

You may also note general comments about your activities as a whole in the General Comments box. In addition, we ask you to indicate anything unusual about your activity during the entry period in the second box. As with the "Other Information/Comments" box associated with each activity, these more general text boxes are intended to provide us with any additional information that may be important to understanding the specific activity information. Again, we strongly encourage their use.

You will be presented with one or two choices for logging out. If you have logged in during the middle of a period, you can submit the current data and return to enter more data for the entry period at a later date by choosing the **Submit Entry and Logout for Now** button. If you know that you will not be doing any more activities during the entry period, choose the **Submit Final Entry for Period** button. Please note that, if you choose this button, you will not be able to enter any further activities for the period or modify data already entered. If you are logging in on the last Friday of an entry period or on any subsequent date, only the **Submit Final Entry for Period** button will appear.

No Work Done

To notify the study that you did no work on any of the statutes or regulations of interest during a specific entry period, select **N/A (no work done)** from the Welcome-Back Page. You should also select this entry if you have previously entered data during the entry period and have done no additional applicable work during the entry period.

Selecting **N/A (no work done)** from the Welcome-Back page will take you to the Review Entries page. Here, you may choose to submit your entry and log out for the time being or submit your final entry for the period (depending on when you are logging in).

System Requirements

The following browsers and platforms are recommended for use with the Empirical Analysis of the Statutory and Regulatory Environment Web Form.

- Microsoft® Windows® 2000:
  - The preferred browser is Microsoft Internet Explorer® 6.x. You may experience minor technical issues with Netscape® 7.x.
- Macintosh® OS X (10.x):
  - The preferred browser is Opera® 6.03. You may experience minor technical issues with Microsoft Internet Explorer 5.2.3 and Netscape 7.x.
- Macintosh OS 9.x:
  - You may experience minor technical issues with Netscape 7.0.

The following browsers and platforms are not recommended for use with the Web form.

- Safari® 1.0 (for Macintosh OS X)
- Microsoft Internet Explorer 5.x (for Macintosh OS 9)
- Netscape 4.x or earlier (for Macintosh and also Windows 2000)

Online Help

Learn more about the study, the kind of information we are interested in obtaining, and technical issues by reviewing the online help pages. The online help pages include an overview of each statutory or regulatory area, examples of "other comments" that might be provided, and key definitions, based on the Defense Acquisition University glossary, *Defense Acquisition Acronyms and Terms*, 11th edition, September 2003.

To review the online help pages, select **Online Help** on the study banner. Links to pop-up windows with definitions for specific activities are located on the activity pages.

Screen Shots of the Web-Based Tool

Below are screen shots of the key Web pages on the data collection protocol Web site.

Contact Information Screen

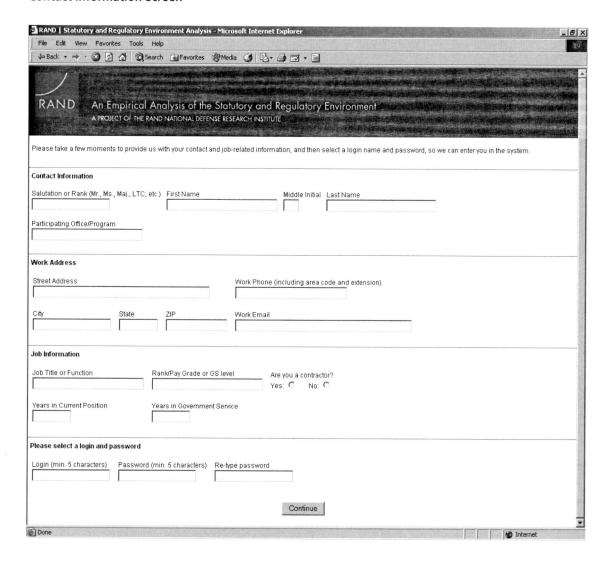

Welcome-Back Page

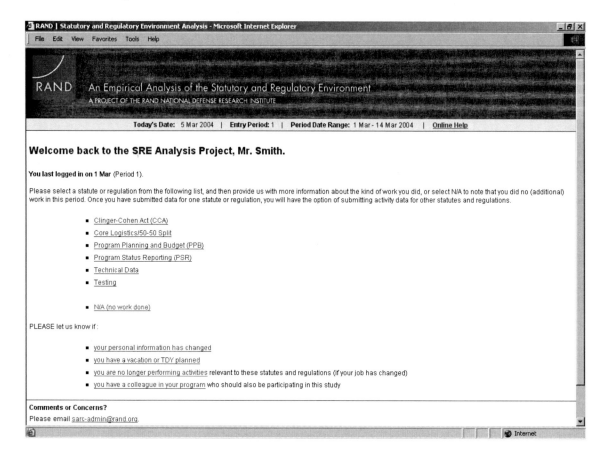

Update Contact Information Screen

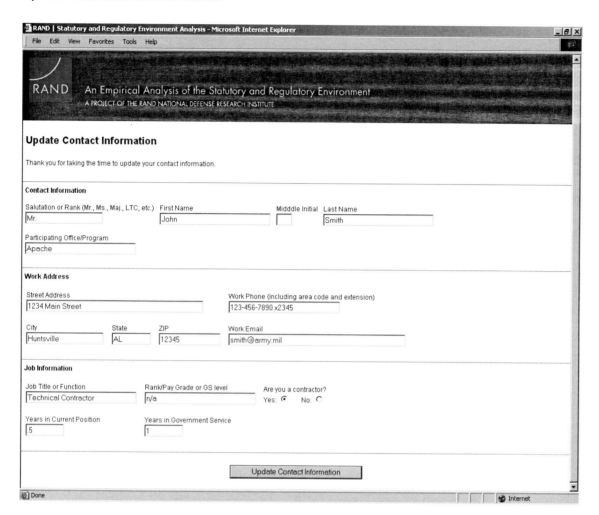

Notification of Vacation or TDY

Notification of Vacation or TDY

Thank you for letting us know in advance of your upcoming vacation or TDY. Please enter the dates you expect to be gone, so we can enter it into the system.

Start Date

End Date

Will anyone be covering for you in your absence?   ○ Yes
○ No
○ Don't know

If yes, please let us know his or her name.

Submit Vacation/TDY Notification

Discontinuing Participation

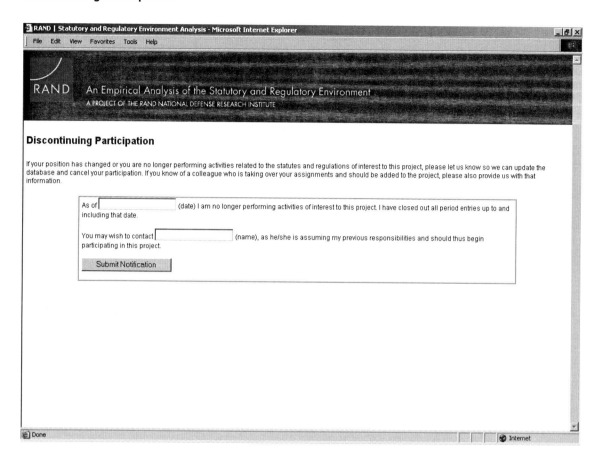

Recommend a Colleague

Clinger-Cohen Act (CCA) Activities Page

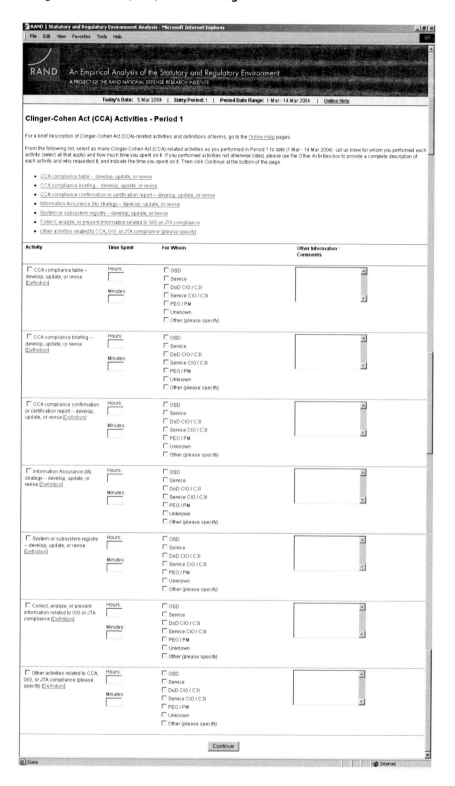

Core Logistics/50-50 Split Activities Page

RAND | Statutory and Regulatory Environment Analysis - Microsoft Internet Explorer

File   Edit   View   Favorites   Tools   Help

RAND   An Empirical Analysis of the Statutory and Regulatory Environment
A PROJECT OF THE RAND NATIONAL DEFENSE RESEARCH INSTITUTE

Today's Date: 5 Mar 2004 | **Entry Period:** 1 | **Period Date Range:** 1 Mar - 14 Mar 2004 | Online Help

Core Logistics/50-50 Split Activities - Period 1

For a brief description of Core Logistics/50-50 Split-related activities and definitions of terms, go to the Online Help pages.

From the following list, select as many Core Logistics/50-50 Split-related activities as you performed in Period 1 to date (1 Mar - 14 Mar 2004). Let us know for whom you performed each activity (select all that apply) and how much time you spent on it. If you performed activities not otherwise listed, please use the Other Activities box to provide a complete description of each activity and who requested it, and indicate the time you spent on it. Then click Continue at the bottom of the page.

- Industrial Capabilities section of the Acquisition Strategy -- develop, update, or revise
- Core/Source of Repair Analysis section of the Acquisition Strategy -- develop, update, or revise
- Competition Analysis section of the Acquisition Strategy -- develop, update, or revise
- Annual 50-50 Depot Maintenance Report to Congress -- develop, update, or revise
- Other activities related to Core Logistics (please specify)

Activity	Time Spent	For Whom	Other Information / Comments
☐ Industrial Capabilities section of the Acquisition Strategy -- develop, update, or revise [Definition]	Hours: Minutes:	☐ OSD ☐ Service ☐ OSD AT&L Staff ☐ Service Acquisition Staff / Functional Office ☐ GAO ☐ PEO / PM ☐ Unknown ☐ Other (please specify)	
☐ Core/Source of Repair Analysis section of the Acquisition Strategy -- develop, update, or revise [Definition]	Hours: Minutes:	☐ OSD ☐ Service ☐ OSD AT&L Staff ☐ Service Acquisition Staff / Functional Office ☐ GAO ☐ PEO / PM ☐ Unknown ☐ Other (please specify)	
☐ Competition Analysis section of the Acquisition Strategy -- develop, update, or revise [Definition]	Hours: Minutes:	☐ OSD ☐ Service ☐ OSD AT&L Staff ☐ Service Acquisition Staff / Functional Office ☐ GAO ☐ PEO / PM ☐ Unknown ☐ Other (please specify)	
☐ Annual 50-50 Depot Maintenance Report to Congress -- develop, update, or revise [Definition]	Hours: Minutes:	☐ OSD ☐ Service ☐ OSD AT&L Staff ☐ Service Acquisition Staff / Functional Office ☐ GAO ☐ PEO / PM ☐ Unknown ☐ Other (please specify)	
☐ Other activities related to Core Logistics (please specify) [Definition]	Hours: Minutes:	☐ OSD ☐ Service ☐ OSD AT&L Staff ☐ Service Acquisition Staff / Functional Office ☐ GAO ☐ PEO / PM ☐ Unknown ☐ Other (please specify)	

Continue

Internet

Program Planning and Budget (PPB) Activities Page

RAND | Statutory and Regulatory Environment Analysis - Microsoft Internet Explorer

File   Edit   View   Favorites   Tools   Help

RAND   An Empirical Analysis of the Statutory and Regulatory Environment
A PROJECT OF THE RAND NATIONAL DEFENSE RESEARCH INSTITUTE

Today's Date: 5 Mar 2004 | **Entry Period:** 1 | **Period Date Range:** 1 Mar - 14 Mar 2004 | Online Help

Program Planning and Budget (PPB) - Period 1

For a brief description of Program Planning and Budget (PPB)-related activities and definitions of terms, go to the Online Help pages.

From the following list, select as many Program Planning and Budget (PPB)-related activities as you performed in Period 1 to date (1 Mar - 14 Mar). Let us know for whom you performed each activity (select all that apply) and how much time you spent on it. If you performed activities not otherwise listed, please use the Other Activities box to provide a complete description of each activity and who requested it, and indicate the time you spent on it. Then click Continue at the bottom of the page.

- Submit an above-threshold reprogramming action
- Submit a below-threshold reprogramming action
- Descope a portion of the program to pay for a funding shortfall elsewhere
- What-if exercise to see the effects of changes in funding, schedule, or quantity
- Other activities related to programming and budgeting (please specify)

Activity	Time Spent	For Whom	Other Information / Comments
☐ Submit an above-threshold reprogramming action [Definition]	Hours: ☐ Minutes: ☐	☐ OSD ☐ Service ☐ Resource Sponsor (Warfighter Community) ☐ Tax or Levy from within the PEO / PM ☐ Unknown ☐ Other (please specify)	
☐ Submit a below-threshold reprogramming action [Definition]	Hours: ☐ Minutes: ☐	☐ OSD ☐ Service ☐ Resource Sponsor (Warfighter Community) ☐ Tax or Levy from within the PEO / PM ☐ Unknown ☐ Other (please specify)	
☐ Descope a portion of the program to pay for a funding shortfall elsewhere [Definition]	Hours: ☐ Minutes: ☐	☐ OSD ☐ Service ☐ Resource Sponsor (Warfighter Community) ☐ Tax or Levy from within the PEO / PM ☐ Unknown ☐ Other (please specify)	
☐ What-if exercise to see the effects of changes in funding, schedule, or quantity [Definition]	Hours: ☐ Minutes: ☐	☐ OSD ☐ Service ☐ Resource Sponsor (Warfighter Community) ☐ Tax or Levy from within the PEO / PM ☐ Unknown ☐ Other (please specify)	
☐ Other activities related to programming and budgeting (please specify) [Definition]	Hours: ☐ Minutes: ☐	☐ OSD ☐ Service ☐ Resource Sponsor (Warfighter Community) ☐ Tax or Levy from within the PEO / PM ☐ Unknown ☐ Other (please specify)	

Continue

Done   Internet

Program Status Reporting (PSR) Activities Page

RAND | Statutory and Regulatory Environment Analysis - Microsoft Internet Explorer

File   Edit   View   Favorites   Tools   Help

RAND   An Empirical Analysis of the Statutory and Regulatory Environment
A PROJECT OF THE RAND NATIONAL DEFENSE RESEARCH INSTITUTE

Today's Date: 5 Mar 2004 | **Entry Period:** 1 | **Period Date Range:** 1 Mar - 14 Mar 2004 | Online Help

Program Status Reporting (PSR) - Period 1

For a brief description of Program Status Reporting (PSR)-related activities and definitions of terms, go to the Online Help pages.

From the following list, select as many Program Status Reporting (PSR)-related activities as you performed in Period 1 to date (1 Mar - 14 Mar). Let us know for whom you performed each activity (select all that apply) and how much time you spent on it. If you performed activities not otherwise listed, please use the Other Activities box to provide a complete description of each activity and who requested it, and indicate the time you spent on it. Then click Continue at the bottom of the page.

- Collect data, prepare, or answer questions related to SAR
- Collect data, prepare, or answer questions related to DAES
- Collect data, prepare, or answer questions related to UCR
- Review, analyze, or forward CCDR
- Collect data, prepare, or answer questions related to APB or ASR
- Other activities relating to cost, schedule, performance, and status reporting (please specify)

Activity	Time Spent	For Whom	Other Information / Comments
☐ Collect data, prepare, or answer questions related to SAR [Definition]	Hours: ___ Minutes: ___	☐ OSD ☐ Service ☐ OSD AT&L Staff ☐ Service Acquisition Staff / Functional Office ☐ PEO / PM ☐ Unknown ☐ Other (please specify)	
☐ Collect data, prepare, or answer questions related to DAES [Definition]	Hours: ___ Minutes: ___	☐ OSD ☐ Service ☐ OSD AT&L Staff ☐ Service Acquisition Staff / Functional Office ☐ PEO / PM ☐ Unknown ☐ Other (please specify)	
☐ Collect data, prepare, or answer questions related to UCR [Definition]	Hours: ___ Minutes: ___	☐ OSD ☐ Service ☐ OSD AT&L Staff ☐ Service Acquisition Staff / Functional Office ☐ PEO / PM ☐ Unknown ☐ Other (please specify)	
☐ Review, analyze, or forward CCDR [Definition]	Hours: ___ Minutes: ___	☐ OSD ☐ Service ☐ OSD AT&L Staff ☐ Service Acquisition Staff / Functional Office ☐ PEO / PM ☐ Unknown ☐ Other (please specify)	
☐ Collect data, prepare, or answer questions related to APB or ASR [Definition]	Hours: ___ Minutes: ___	☐ OSD ☐ Service ☐ OSD AT&L Staff ☐ Service Acquisition Staff / Functional Office ☐ PEO / PM ☐ Unknown ☐ Other (please specify)	
☐ Other activities relating to cost, schedule, performance, and status reporting (please specify) [Definition]	Hours: ___ Minutes: ___	☐ OSD ☐ Service ☐ OSD AT&L Staff ☐ Service Acquisition Staff / Functional Office ☐ PEO / PM ☐ Unknown ☐ Other (please specify)	

[Continue]

Internet

Technical Data Activities Page

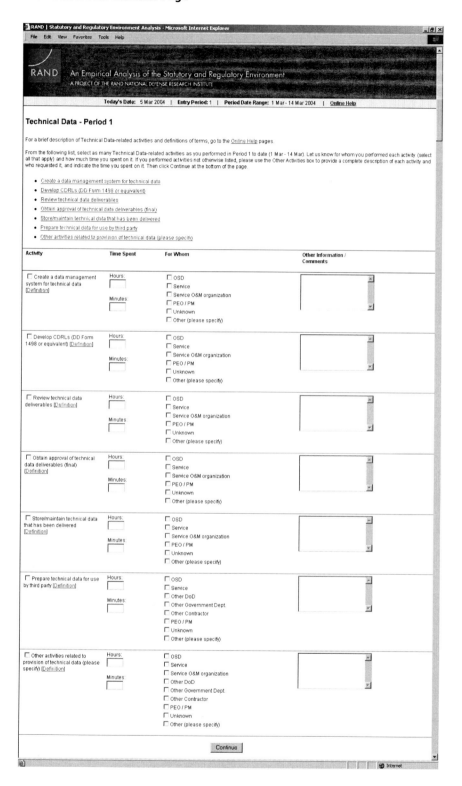

Testing Activities Page (Screen One)

RAND | Statutory and Regulatory Environment Analysis - Microsoft Internet Explorer

File   Edit   View   Favorites   Tools   Help

RAND   An Empirical Analysis of the Statutory and Regulatory Environment
A PROJECT OF THE RAND NATIONAL DEFENSE RESEARCH INSTITUTE

Today's Date: 5 Mar 2004 | Entry Period: 1 | Period Date Range: 1 Mar - 14 Mar 2004 | Online Help

Testing Activities - Period 1

For a brief description of Testing-related activities and definitions of terms, go to the Online Help pages.

From the following list, select as many Testing-related activities as you performed in Period 1 to date (1 Mar - 14 Mar). Let us know for whom you performed each activity (select all that apply) and how much time you spent on it. If you performed activities not otherwise listed, please use the Other Activities box to provide a complete description of each activity and who requested it, and indicate the time you spent on it. Then click Continue at the bottom of the page.

The testing activities to be captured are those related to Major Defense Acquisition Programs (MDAPs) and other major acquisition efforts (ACAT II) currently on the Director, Operational Test and Evaluation Oversight list. Please only report time spent on these programs managed within your project office.

- Annual Report of DOT&E (Director, Operational Test and Evaluation) -- develop, update, or revise
- Review Requirements Document (please state document)
- TEMP -- develop, update, or revise
- Beyond LRIP Report -- develop, update, or revise
- Operational Test Plan -- develop, update, or revise
- LRIP/IOT&E Brief -- develop, update, or revise
- FRP Brief -- develop, update, or revise
- Operational Test Readiness Review (OTRR) -- develop, update, or revise
- Review Live Fire Test Plan/Strategy
- Obtain Live Fire Waiver
- Other activities related to operational and live-fire testing (please specify)

Activity	Time Spent	For Whom	Other Information / Comments
☐ Annual Report of DOT&E (Director, Operational Test and Evaluation) -- develop, update, or revise [Definition]	Hours: ☐	☐ OSD ☐ Service ☐ DOT&E ☐ Service Testing Oversight Agency ☐ Operational Test Agency ☐ PEO / PM ☐ Unknown ☐ Other (please specify)	
	Minutes: ☐		
☐ Review Requirements Document (please state document) [Definition]	Hours: ☐	☐ OSD ☐ Service ☐ DOT&E ☐ Service Testing Oversight Agency ☐ Operational Test Agency ☐ PEO / PM ☐ Unknown ☐ Other (please specify)	
	Minutes: ☐		
☐ TEMP -- develop, update, or revise [Definition]	Hours: ☐	☐ OSD ☐ Service ☐ DOT&E ☐ Service Testing Oversight Agency ☐ Operational Test Agency ☐ PEO / PM ☐ Unknown ☐ Other (please specify)	
	Minutes: ☐		
☐ Beyond LRIP Report -- develop, update, or revise [Definition]	Hours: ☐	☐ OSD ☐ Service ☐ DOT&E ☐ Service Testing Oversight Agency ☐ Operational Test Agency ☐ PEO / PM ☐ Unknown ☐ Other (please specify)	
	Minutes: ☐		

Testing Activities Page (Screen Two)

☐ Operational Test Plan -- develop, update, or revise [Definition]	Hours: ☐ Minutes: ☐	☐ OSD ☐ Service ☐ DOT&E ☐ Service Testing Oversight Agency ☐ Operational Test Agency ☐ PEO / PM ☐ Unknown ☐ Other (please specify)	
☐ LRIP/IOT&E Brief -- develop, update, or revise [Definition]	Hours: ☐ Minutes: ☐	☐ OSD ☐ Service ☐ DOT&E ☐ Service Testing Oversight Agency ☐ Operational Test Agency ☐ PEO / PM ☐ Unknown ☐ Other (please specify)	
☐ FRP Brief -- develop, update, or revise [Definition]	Hours: ☐ Minutes: ☐	☐ OSD ☐ Service ☐ DOT&E ☐ Service Testing Oversight Agency ☐ Operational Test Agency ☐ PEO / PM ☐ Unknown ☐ Other (please specify)	
☐ Operational Test Readiness Review (OTRR) -- develop, update, or revise [Definition]	Hours: ☐ Minutes: ☐	☐ OSD ☐ Service ☐ DOT&E ☐ Service Testing Oversight Agency ☐ Operational Test Agency ☐ PEO / PM ☐ Unknown ☐ Other (please specify)	
☐ Review Live Fire Test Plan/Strategy [Definition]	Hours: ☐ Minutes: ☐	☐ OSD ☐ Service ☐ DOT&E ☐ Service Testing Oversight Agency ☐ Operational Test Agency ☐ PEO / PM ☐ Unknown ☐ Other (please specify)	
☐ Obtain Live Fire Waiver [Definition]	Hours: ☐ Minutes: ☐	☐ OSD ☐ Service ☐ DOT&E ☐ Service Testing Oversight Agency ☐ Operational Test Agency ☐ PEO / PM ☐ Unknown ☐ Other (please specify)	
☐ Other activities related to operational and live-fire testing (please specify) [Definition]	Hours: ☐ Minutes: ☐	☐ OSD ☐ Service ☐ DOT&E ☐ Service Testing Oversight Agency ☐ Operational Test Agency ☐ PEO / PM ☐ Unknown ☐ Other (please specify)	

[Continue]

Internet

List of Statutes and Regulations

This page is seen after clicking **Continue** on an Activities page.

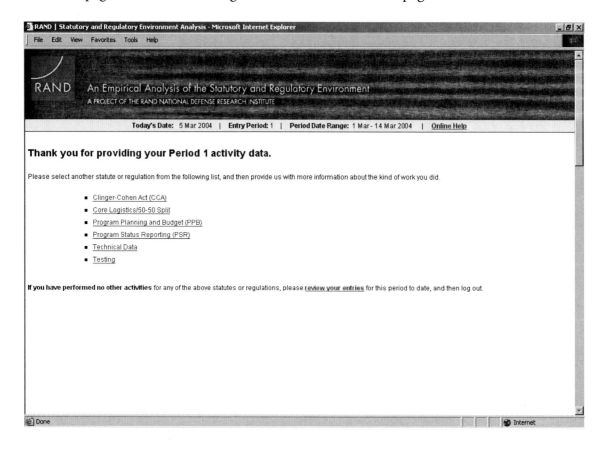

Review Entries Page

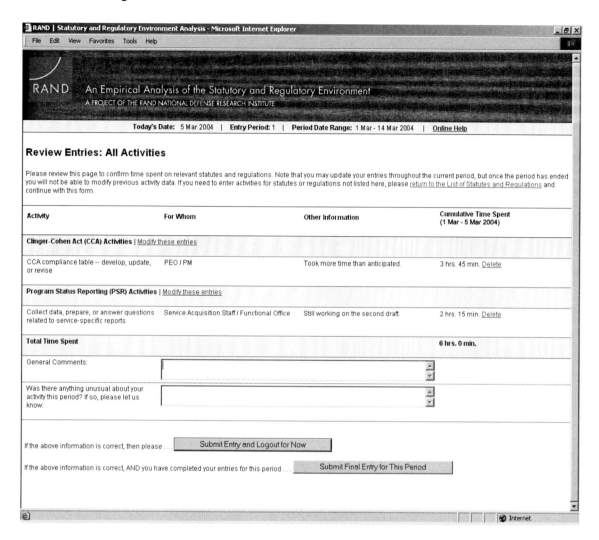

RAND   An Empirical Analysis of the Statutory and Regulatory Environment
A PROJECT OF THE RAND NATIONAL DEFENSE RESEARCH INSTITUTE

Today's Date: 5 Mar 2004 | Entry Period: 1 | Period Date Range: 1 Mar - 14 Mar 2004 | Online Help

Review Entries: All Activities

Please review this page to confirm time spent on relevant statutes and regulations. Note that you may update your entries throughout the current period, but once the period has ended you will not be able to modify previous activity data. If you need to enter activities for statutes or regulations not listed here, please return to the List of Statutes and Regulations and continue with this form.

Activity	For Whom	Other Information	Cumulative Time Spent (1 Mar - 5 Mar 2004)
Clinger-Cohen Act (CCA) Activities | Modify these entries			
CCA compliance table -- develop, update, or revise	PEO / PM	Took more time than anticipated.	3 hrs. 45 min. Delete
Program Status Reporting (PSR) Activities | Modify these entries			
Collect data, prepare, or answer questions related to service-specific reports	Service Acquisition Staff / Functional Office	Still working on the second draft.	2 hrs. 15 min. Delete
Total Time Spent			**6 hrs. 0 min.**
General Comments:			
Was there anything unusual about your activity this period? If so, please let us know:			

If the above information is correct, then please ...   [Submit Entry and Logout for Now]

If the above information is correct, AND you have completed your entries for this period ...   [Submit Final Entry for This Period]

Internet

Definitions and Descriptions of Activities Under the Five Areas

The following information describing and defining each of the five statutory and regulatory areas of interest appeared on the data collection protocol Web site.

Clinger-Cohen Act (CCA)

Clinger-Cohen Act–related activities refer to provisions in the Information Technology Management Reform Act 1996 (ITMRA; Division E of the FY 1996 National Defense Authorization Act) that set rules (provisions) for the management of information systems and technology in federal agencies, including DoD. In general, most weapon systems meet the definition of a National Security System contained in the act, and so must comply with the law's provisions, as implemented through DoD policy (DoD Instruction 5000.2). Also included are the provisions in PL 105-261, Subtitle D (National Defense Authorization Act 1999), which sets additional responsibilities for the CIO.

Any and all activities undertaken at the program level to comply with CCA or related DoD policy and implementation guidance associated with managing information technology and resources, including the Global Information Grid (GIG) and the Joint Technical Architecture (JTA), need to be included. This includes activities related to the Information Technology Acquisition Board.

Definitions
The following definitions are excerpted from the *Glossary of Defense Acquisition Acronyms and Terms*, 11th edition (2003) and DoD Instruction 5000.2 of May 12, 2003:

> **Clinger-Cohen Act (CCA)** Consists of Division D and Division E of the 1996 National Defense Authorization Act (NDAA). Division D is the Federal Acquisition Reform Act (FARA) and Division E is the Information Technology Management Reform Act (ITMRA). Both divisions of the act made significant changes to defense acquisition policy. (*Glossary of Defense Acquisition Acronyms and Terms*, 2003, p. B-20)

> **Clinger-Cohen Act (CCA) Certification** Requirement for Major Automated Information Systems (MAISs) [stating] that a Milestone Decision Authority not grant Milestone B

approval until the Component Head or designee confirms to the DoD Chief Information Officer (CIO) that the system is being developed in accordance with the CCA. (*Glossary of Defense Acquisition Acronyms and Terms, 2003*, p. B-20).

Global Information Grid (GIG) The globally interconnected, end-to-end set of information capabilities, associated processes, and personnel for collecting, processing, storing, disseminating, and managing information on demand to warfighters, policy makers, and support personnel. The GIG includes all owned and leased communications and computing systems and services, software (including applications), data, security services, and other associated services necessary to achieve information superiority. It also includes National Security Systems . . . as defined in Section 5142 of the Clinger-Cohen Act (CCA) of 1996. (CJCSI 6212.01B) (*Glossary of Defense Acquisition Acronyms and Terms*, 2003, p. B-62)

Information Technology Management Reform Act (ITMRA) Division E of the 1996 NDAA. It repealed the Brooks Act, defined Information Technology (IT) and National Security Systems (NSSs), established the requirement to designate a Chief Information Officer (CIO) for each major Federal Agency, assigned the responsibility for management of IT to the Director, Office of Management and Budget (OMB), and moved procurement protest authority from the General Services Administration (GSA) to the [General Accounting Office] (GAO). [It is f]requently, but erroneously, referred to as the Clinger-Cohen Act (CCA). (*Glossary of Defense Acquisition Acronyms and Terms*, 2003, p. B-70)

Joint Technical Architecture (JTA) A common set of mandatory Information Technology (IT) standards (primarily interface standards) and guidelines to be used by all emerging systems and systems upgrades including Advanced Concept Technology Demonstrations (ACTDs). The JTA can be used to establish a system's technical architecture and is applicable to all Command, Control, Communications, Computers, and Intelligence (C4I) and Automated Information Systems (AISs) and the interfaces of other key assets (e.g., weapon systems, sensors) with C4I systems. (*Glossary of Defense Acquisition Acronyms and Terms*, 2003, pp. B-77–B-78)

National Security System (NSS) Any telecommunications or information system operated by the United States Government, . . . the function, operation, or use of which involves intelligence activities, cryptologic activities related to national security, command and control of military systems, equipment that is an integral part of a [weapon] system, or is critical to the fulfillment of military or intelligence missions. (*Glossary of Defense Acquisition Acronyms and Terms*, 2003, p. B-93; see also PL 104-106, Division E, Sec. 5142)

Information Technology Acquisition Board (ITAB). [Advises] the . . . DoD CIO on critical acquisition decisions. These reviews . . . enable the execution of the DoD CIO's acquisition-related responsibilities for IT, including NSS, under the Clinger-Cohen Act (CCA), reference (l), and Title 10 of the United States Code, reference (m). (DoD Instruction 5000.2, para. 3.10.3)

Chief Information Officer (CIO) An executive agency official responsible for providing advice and other assistance to the head of the executive agency to ensure that Information Technology (IT) is acquired and information resources are managed for the executive agency according to statute; developing, maintaining, and facilitating the implementation of a sound and integrated Information Technology Architecture (ITA) for the executive agency; and promoting the effective and efficient design and operation of all major information resources management processes for the executive agency, including improvements to work processes of the executive agency. The CIO for DoD is the Assistant Secretary of Defense for Networks and Information Integration (ASD[NII]). (*Glossary of Defense Acquisition Acronyms and Terms*, 2003, p. B-20)

C4I (Command, Control, Communications, Computers, and Intelligence) Support Plan (C4ISP) A requirement for all Acquisition Category (ACAT) programs that connect . . . to the communications and information infrastructure, and includes both Information Technology (IT) systems and National Security System (NSS) programs. The plan identifies Command, Control, Communications, Computers, Intelligence, Surveillance, and Reconnaissance (C4ISR) needs, dependencies, and interfaces focusing attention on interoperability, supportability, and sufficiency concerns throughout a program's life cycle. (*Glossary of Defense Acquisition Acronyms and Terms*, 2003, p. B-18)

Information Assurance (IA) Information operations that protect and defend information and information systems by ensuring their availability, integrity, authentication, confidentiality, and non-repudiation. This includes providing for the restoration of information systems by incorporating protection, detection, and reaction capabilities. (CJCSI 3170.01C) (*Glossary of Defense Acquisition Acronyms and Terms*, 2003, p. B-68–B-69)

Descriptions of Activities

Develop, update, or revise CCA compliance table. A compliance table is a table, prepared by the program office, indicating which acquisition documents correspond to CCA requirements. The documents identified in the table are used to assess and confirm CCA compliance (see DoDI 5000.2, para. E4.2.2; example table, E4.T1).

Develop, update, or revise CCA compliance briefing. A compliance briefing is a presentation documenting a program's compliance with CCA and related IT provisions. Its intended audiences include DoD and Service CIOs, and OSD or Service functional staff with acquisition or IT-related oversight responsibilities.

Develop, update, or revise CCA compliance confirmation or certification report. The compliance confirmation or certification report is written confirmation by the DoD CIO or Component CIO that a program is in compliance with applicable provisions of CCA or related IT statutory and regulatory provisions. Confirmation applies to all MDAPs; formal certification applies to Major Automated Information Systems only (see DoDI 5000.2, para. E4.2.2).

Develop, update, or revise Information Assurance (IA) strategy. IA strategy is a strategy to protect and defend information and information systems by ensuring their availability, integrity, authentication, confidentiality, and non-repudiation. An IA strategy, consistent with the GIG and other DoD policies, standards, and architectures, is a required document to confirm or certify CCA compliance (see DoDI 5000.2, Table E4.T1).

Develop, update, or revise system or subsystem registry. System registration involves the registration of mission-critical and mission-essential information systems (PL 107-248, Sec. 8088; see also DoDI 5000.2, Table E3.T1).

Collect, analyze, or present information related to GIG or JTA compliance. JTA- and GIG-related activities are those activities that focus on determining and meeting IT architecture, connectivity (interface standards), interoperability, or information flow requirements.

Other activities related to CCA, GIG, or JTA compliance (please specify). This includes any activity related to managing a program's information technology and systems that does not fall under the activities listed earlier. It may include special requests for information, support for ITAB decisions, determining interoperability requirements, obtaining interoperability certification, or developing or updating the C4ISP.

Core Logistics/50-50 Split

The Core logistics capability requirement and the 50-50 depot maintenance requirement are laid out in 10 USC 2464 and 10 USC 2466. At the program office level, this includes any activities undertaken to collect, monitor, or report data or other information regarding the maintenance needs of a weapon system. Many of these activities support the logistics or maintenance sections of a program's Acquisition Strategy Report or are required to support decisions regarding the support plan for a system. For example, time spent reallocating funding in order to meet the 50-50 criteria should be reported. On the other hand, time spent dealing with reprogramming or new budgeting actions, even when they involve the funding for depot maintenance, need to be reported in the Program Planning and Budgeting area.

Definitions

Core logistics capability. The capability maintained within organic defense depots to meet the readiness and sustainability requirements of weapon systems that support Joint Chiefs of Staff contingency scenarios.

50-50 split. The requirement that 50 percent of the funding for depot-level maintenance and repair given to each of the Services and defense agencies must be spent on work at government facilities.

Depot-level maintenance. Maintenance performed on materiel requiring major overhaul or a complete rebuild of parts, assemblies, subassemblies, and end items, including the manufacture of parts, modification, testing, and reclamation, as required. It supports organizational and intermediate maintenance activities by more-extensive shop facilities and personnel of higher technical skill than are normally available at the lower levels of maintenance.

Acquisition strategy. A business and technical management approach designed to achieve program objectives within the resource constraints imposed by the current regulatory environment. It is the framework for planning, directing, contracting for, and managing a program. It provides a master schedule for research, development, test, production, fielding, modification, postproduction management, and other activities essential for program success. The acquisition strategy is the basis for formulating functional plans and strategies (e.g., TEMP, Acquisition Plan, competition, systems engineering, among others).

Industrial capabilities analysis. DoD must give "consideration of the national technology and industrial base in the development and implementation of acquisition plans for each major defense acquisition program" (10 USC 2440).

Core logistics analysis/source of repair analysis. DoD must "maintain a core logistics capability that is Government-owned and Government-operated" in order to maintain and repair weapon systems and other military equipment that is "necessary to enable the armed forces to fulfill the strategic and contingency plans prepared by the Chairman of the Joint Chiefs of Staff" (10 USC 2464, subsection [a] para. [1], paragraph [3]).

Competition analysis. Any depot-level maintenance and repair spending in excess of $3 million may be contracted out only if DoD uses "(1) merit-based selection procedures for competitions among all depot-level activities of the Department of Defense; or (2) competitive procedures for competitions among private and public sector entities" (10 USC 2469, subsection [a], para. [1] and [2]).

Descriptions of Activities

Develop, update, or revise industrial capabilities section of the acquisition strategy. These are activities related to industrial capabilities analysis (defined earlier).

Develop, update, or revise core/source of repair analysis section of the acquisition strategy. These are activities related to core logistics/source of repair analysis (defined earlier).

Develop, update, or revise competition analysis section of the acquisition strategy. These are activities related to competition analysis (defined earlier).

Develop, update, or revise annual 50-50 Depot Maintenance Report to Congress. Each year DoD must submit reports identifying, for each Service and each defense agency, the percentage of funds that were expended for depot-level maintenance and repair by the public and private sectors for the preceding two fiscal years and for the subsequent five fiscal years (10 USC 2466).

Other activities related to core logistics (please specify). Examples of possible entries include:

- GAO is doing a study on how current acquisition programs are meeting the core logistics requirement and asks you to brief it on your program. Time spent preparing and delivering the briefing should be reported in this category.
- As part of a Service-wide effort to improve business practices, the Office of the Service Secretary asks each program to produce current and historical data and graphs on how depot spending has changed over the life of the program. Time spent producing new graphs or putting existing data into new forms should be reported in this category.

Program Planning and Budgeting

The programming and budgeting processes within the Department of Defense are both complex and time consuming. Because a Service or agency balances its total resource plan when submitting either a POM or a budget, priorities for resources are not always clear to those in the chain of command. This set of activities, in response to many in the acquisition process, is intended to capture the time taken by program personnel professionals (and hence the cost to the program) to respond to the specific requests for program or budget information.

Definitions

Programming. The projection of activities to be accomplished and the resources that will be required for specified periods in the future, normally six years. It involves the process of estimating and requesting resources for a program, especially in terms of quantitative requirements for funding manpower, material, and facilities for program office operations and for the design, development, and production of a defense weapon system.

Reprogramming. The transfer of funds between program elements or time lines within an appropriation for purpose other than those intended at the time of appropriation. Reprogramming is generally accomplished pursuant to consultation with, and approval by, appropriate congressional committees if above-thresholds are prescribed for various appropriations (i.e., procurement; military construction; operation and maintenance; military personnel; and research, development, test, and evaluation). Reprogramming refers to the activity intended to move money between accounts; the problem is often described as a "color of money" issue wherein the "colors" correspond to budget accounts.

"Color of money." Color of money is a term that refers to the challenges generated because program funding is provided in specific budget accounts, each with specific constraints on how that money can be spent. In the acquisition process, for example, there is often a need during the research, test, and development portion of the program to increase the RDT&E account by using funds from either procurement or operations and maintenance. This kind of problem is often referred to as a color of money problem. There are two ways in which this transfer can take place: (1) if below the current congressional threshold for RDT&E (up to $10 million), monies from other RDT&E accounts can be transferred into the account in question; or (2) if above the threshold amount, or if the threshold has already been met, a reprogramming request can be submitted to Congress for the transfer of funds into the account in question from any other appropriation so indicated on the reprogramming transfer request. Of course, this request must be reviewed by the Service comptroller, the OSD comptroller, and others on its way to Congress, and these requests are usually packaged together and submitted late in the fiscal year.

What-if exercises. These are budget exercises undertaken to assess the impact of changes in funding, schedule, or quantity. The source of such change may be external to the program office (e.g., congressional markup language, OSD comptroller decision).

Descriptions of Activities

Plan, prepare, or submit an above-threshold reprogramming action. This activity relates to the color of money phenomenon and is intended to capture time spent planning, preparing, or executing an above-threshold reprogramming action. Any movement of funds from one appropriation account to another, or from one program element to another within an appropriation, that is above a particular threshold ($10 million for RDT&E or $20 million for procurement) is considered an "above-threshold reprogramming action" and requires the approval of Congress. For a Service (or department) to obtain an above-threshold reprogramming action, it must submit the request through its comptroller and the OSD comptroller to the Senate and House Armed Services Committees as well as to the Defense Subcommittees of the Senate and House Appropriations Committees. All four committees must approve the action and, most importantly, the offsets proposed by the Service (or department).

Plan, prepare, or submit a below-threshold reprogramming action. This activity relates to the general color of money phenomenon and is intended to capture time spent planning, preparing, or executing a below-threshold reprogramming action. A below-threshold reprogramming action refers to an informal agreement between committee staffers of the Senate and House Armed Services Committees and the Defense Subcommittees of the Senate and House Appropriations Committees to permit DoD to move small amounts of funding among certain appropriations without the notification or approval of Congress. These thresholds differ for various appropriations: For example, current thresholds are up to $10 million of RDT&E funds and up to $20 million in procurement funds within the same account.

Descope a portion of the program to pay for a funding shortfall elsewhere. This usually occurs at the request of the program manager or program executive officer. When a portion of a program requires additional funds (because of a problem in testing, for example), funds may be moved from one portion of a program to another, within the same appropriation. Using procurement funds as an example, descoping might involve funding spare parts with monies originally set aside for test equipment. In R&D, this may involve moving monies from a test article to the testing regime itself. What distinguishes this from above- or below-threshold reprogramming is that it is done at the local or program level and does not require OSD or congressional knowledge or approval.

What-if exercise to see the effects of changes in funding, schedule, or quantity. During the programming process or, to a lesser extent, the budgeting process, community sponsors and programming officials tend to ask "what-if" questions. For example, "What if I reduce the quantity of the system from X per year to Y per year? What would be the effect on unit cost?" Or, "What if we move the initial operational capability from year X to year Y?" These questions naturally arise as people try to balance the budgets and programs in these processes. It is usually incumbent upon the program office to provide these estimates rather than have people with little understanding of the program dynamics provide them.

Other activities related to programming and budgeting (please specify). This is a catch-all category to cover any financial, programming, or budget-related activity not included in the above categories.

Program Status Reporting

This section addresses key reporting requirements provided on a regular or one-time basis by the program office to a variety of sponsors, including OSD(AT&L), Congress, and Services, among others. We have included the SAR, DAES, UCR, CCDR, APB, and ASR in this section. There are also Service-specific monthly status reports or reports responding to inquiries on current program cost, schedule, and performance issues from a variety of sponsors. These could be included under the "other activities relating to cost, schedule, performance, and status reporting" category

Definitions

Selected Acquisition Report (SAR). A standard, comprehensive, summary status report of a Major Defense Acquisition Program (MDAP) (Acquisition Category [ACAT] I) required for annual submission to Congress. It includes key cost, schedule, and technical information.

Defense Acquisition Executive Summary (DAES). The principal OSD mechanism of tracking programs between milestone reviews. A DAES report is provided by the program manager of a Major Defense Acquisition Program (MDAP) to USD[AT&L] each calendar quarter.

Unit Cost Report (UCR). Submitted by the program manager of an MDAP (other than a program not required to be included in the SAR for that quarter) on a quarterly basis to the Service Acquisition Executive (SAE) providing unit costs of the program with the following information:

1. Program acquisition unit cost
2. Procurement unit cost (in the case of a procurement program)
3. Any cost or schedule variance in a major contract under the program since the contract was executed
4. Any changes from program schedule milestones or program performances reflected in the baseline description that are known, expected, or anticipated by the program manager
5. Additionally, during a quarter, the project manager notifies the SAE with the above information any time there is reasonable cause to believe that the program acquisition or procurement unit cost has increased by 15 percent over the baseline estimate.

Contractor Cost Data Reporting (CCDR). The contractor provides this report, which contains the actual costs of all the activities incurred by the contractor during the reporting period, to the program office. The main purpose of the CCDR is to serve as a primary contract cost database for most DoD cost estimating efforts internal and external to the program.

Acquisition Program Baseline (APB). Prescribes the key cost, schedule, and performance targets in the phase succeeding the milestone for which it was developed. This baseline has key performance parameters (KPP), which are the minimum attributes or characteristics considered most essential for an effective military capability.

Acquisition Strategy Report (ASR). This report provides a business and technical management approach designed to achieve program objectives within the imposed resource constraints. It is the framework for planning, directing, contracting for, and managing a program. It provides a master schedule for research, development, test, production, fielding, modification, postproduction management, and other activities essential for program success.

Descriptions of Activities

Collect data, prepare, or answer questions related to SAR. These are activities related to SAR (defined earlier).

Collect data, prepare, or answer questions related to DAES. These are activities related to DAES (defined earlier).

Collect data, prepare, or answer questions related to UCR. These are activities related to UCR (defined earlier).

Review, analyze, or forward CCDR. These are activities related to CCDR (defined earlier).

Collect data, prepare, or answer questions related to APB or ASR. These are activities related to APB or ASR (defined earlier).

Collect data, prepare, or answer questions related to Service-specific reports. Each Service has its own reporting requirements for acquisition programs. The Army uses the Army Acquisition Information System, the Navy its Dashboard, and the Air Force its SMARTT (System Metrics and Reporting Tool). There may be other reporting required by individual PEOs or the military Services; they should be accounted for in this area of the form.

Other activities relating to cost, schedule, performance, and status reporting (please specify). Any activity related to reporting program status that does not fall under the activities listed above. Other activities could include, for example, responding to inquiries on current program cost, schedule, and performance issues from GAO or other congressional organizations, DoD organizations not part of the acquisition community (e.g., PA&E), or nongovernmental organizations.

Testing

This area is intended to capture the effort of program office staff in managing test efforts, planning tests, and utilizing test results for key decisionmakers involved in leading major defense acquisition programs. Testing activities directly rooted in statute, and thus only those major defense acquisition programs receiving oversight (as listed on the DOT&E oversight list), need to be included in the data collection effort.

If testing-related events cause a change in schedule or budget, the level of effort reallocating resources must be reported under the Program Planning and Budget (PPB) area.

Since testing and system requirements are so interrelated, only the time spent in requirements review and updating requirement documents (ICD, CDD, CPD) related to testing (e.g., requirement modifications due to test-identified shortfalls, clarification of vague or untestable requirements, etc.) needs to be captured.

Definitions

The following definitions are excerpted from the *Glossary of Defense Acquisition Acronyms and Terms*, 11th edition (2003); DoD Instruction 5000.2 of May 12, 2003; and Secretary of the Navy Instruction 5000.2B of December 6, 1996:

Test and Evaluation Master Plan (TEMP) Documents the overall structure and objectives of the Test and Evaluation (T&E) program. It provides a framework within which to generate detailed T&E plans and it documents schedule and resource implications associated with the T&E program. The TEMP identifies the necessary Developmental Test and Evaluation (DT&E), Operational Test and Evaluation (OT&E), and Live Fire Test and Evaluation (LFT&E) activities. It relates program schedule, test management strategy and structure, and required resources to: Critical Operational Issues (COIs), Critical Technical Parameters (CTPs), objectives and thresholds documented in the Capability Development Document (CDD), evaluation criteria, and milestone decision points. For multi-Service or joint programs, a single integrated TEMP is required. Component-unique content requirements, particularly evaluation criteria associated with COIs, can be addressed in a component-prepared annex to the basic TEMP. (*Glossary of Defense Acquisition Acronyms and Terms*, 2003, p. B-142)

Low Rate Initial Production (LRIP) 1. The first effort of the Production and Deployment (P&D) phase. The purpose of this effort is to establish an initial production base for the system, permit an orderly ramp-up sufficient to lead to a smooth transition to Full Rate Production (FRP), and to provide production representative articles for Initial Operational Test and Evaluation (IOT&E) and full-up live fire testing. This effort concludes with a Full Rate Production Decision Review (FRPDR) to authorize Full Rate Production and Deployment (FRP&D). 2. The minimum number of systems (other than ships and satellites) to provide production representative articles for Operational Test and Evaluation (OT&E), to establish an initial production base, and to permit an orderly increase in the production rate sufficient to lead to Full Rate Production (FRP) upon successful completion of Operational Testing (OT). For Major Defense Acquisition Programs (MDAPs), LRIP quantities in excess of 10 percent of the acquisition objective must be reported in the Selected Acquisition Report (SAR). For ships and satellites LRIP is the minimum quantity and rate that preserves mobilization. (*Glossary of Defense Acquisition Acronyms and Terms*, 2003, p. B-82–B-83)

Initial Operational Test and Evaluation (IOT&E) Dedicated Operational Test and Evaluation (OT&E) conducted on production, or production representative articles, to determine whether systems are operationally effective and suitable, and . . . supports the decision to proceed Beyond Low Rate Initial Production (BLRIP). (*Glossary of Defense Acquisition Acronyms and Terms*, 2003, p. B-71)

Full-Rate Production and Deployment. Continuation into full-rate production results from a successful Full-Rate Production Decision Review by the MDA (or person designated by the MDA). This effort delivers the fully funded quantity of systems and supporting materiel and services for the program or increment to the users. During this effort, units shall attain Initial Operational Capability. (DoD Instruction 5000.2, para. 3.8.5)

[Operational Test Readiness Review (OTRR) Navy procedure for] certifying readiness for OT&E. The [Systems Command, PEO, and Program Manager will] convene an operational test readiness review. . . . This review shall include all members of the testing team (DT&E and OT&E) and include representatives from [the Service Test and Evaluation Oversight], program sponsor, and [Operational Test Agency]. (SECNAV Instruction 5000.2B, para. 3.4.3.3)

Milestone Decision Authority (MDA) Designated individual with overall responsibility for a program. The MDA shall have the authority to approve entry of an acquisition program into the next phase of the acquisition process and shall be accountable for cost, schedule, and performance reporting to higher authority, including congressional reporting. (*Glossary of Defense Acquisition Acronyms and Terms*, 2003, p. B-89)

[Service Acquisition Executive (SAE)] Secretaries of the Military Departments or Heads of Agencies with the power of redelegation. In the Military Departments, the officials delegated as [SAEs] . . . are, respectively, the Assistant Secretary of the Army (Acquisition, Logistics, and Technology) (ASA[AL&T]), the Assistant Secretary of the Navy (Research, Development, and Acquisition) (ASN[RD&A]), and the Assistant Secretary of the Air Force (Acquisition) (ASAF[A]). [The] SAEs for the Military Departments and acquisition executives in other DoD Components, such as the U.S. Special Operations Command (USSOCOM) and Defense Logistics Agency (DLA) . . . also have acquisition management responsibilities. (*Glossary of Defense Acquisition Acronyms and Terms*, 2003, see DoD Component Acquisition Executive, p. B-45)

Program Executive Officer . . . A military or civilian official who has responsibility for directing several Major Defense Acquisition Programs (MDAPs) and for assigned major system and non-major system acquisition programs. A [Program Executive Officer] has no other command or staff responsibilities within the component, and only reports to and receives guidance and direction from the DoD [Service Acquisition Executive]. (*Glossary of Defense Acquisition Acronyms and Terms*, 2003, pp. B-112–B-113)

Operational Test Agency. The following Service organizations are responsible for operational testing:

- AFOTEC (Air Force Operational Test and Evaluation Center)
- ATEC (Army Test and Evaluation Command)
- COMOPTEVFOR (Navy Commander Operational Test and Evaluation Force)
- MCOTEA (Marine Corps Operational Test and Evaluation Activity)

[Director, Operational Test and Evaluation (DOT&E)] There is a Director of Operational Test and Evaluation in the Department of Defense, appointed from civilian life by the President, by and with the advice and consent of the Senate. The Director shall be appointed without regard to political affiliation and solely on the basis of fitness to perform the duties of the office of Director. . . . The Director is the principal adviser to the Secretary of Defense and the Under Secretary of Defense for Acquisition, Technology, and Logistics on operational test and evaluation in the Department of Defense and the principal operational test and evaluation official within the senior management of the Department of Defense. The Director shall—

(1) prescribe, by authority of the Secretary of Defense, policies and procedures for the conduct of operational test and evaluation in the Department of Defense;

(2) provide guidance to and consult with the Secretary of Defense and the Under Secretary of Defense for Acquisition, Technology, and Logistics and the Secretaries of the military departments with respect to operational test and evaluation in the Department of Defense in general and with respect to specific operational test and evaluation to be conducted in connection with a major defense acquisition program;

(3) monitor and review all operational test and evaluation in the Department of Defense;

(4) coordinate operational testing conducted jointly by more than one military department or defense agency;

(5) review and make recommendations to the Secretary of Defense on all budgetary and financial matters relating to operational test and evaluation, including operational test facilities and equipment, in the Department of Defense; and

(6) monitor and review the live fire testing activities of the Department of Defense provided for under section 2366 of this title. (10 USC 139)

[Beyond Low Rate Initial Production Report (BLRIP)] A final decision within the Department of Defense to proceed with a major defense acquisition program beyond low-rate initial production may not be made until the [Director, Operational Test and Evaluation] has submitted to the Secretary of Defense the report with respect to that program . . . and the congressional defense committees have received that report. (10 USC 2399, subsection [b], para. [4])

[Live Fire Test and Evaluation (LFT&E)] [A] covered system may not proceed beyond low-rate initial production until realistic survivability testing of the system is completed in accordance with [10 USC 2366] and the report required by [10 USC 2366, subsection (d)] with respect to that testing is submitted. . . . [A] major munitions program or a missile program may not proceed beyond low-rate initial production until realistic lethality testing of the program is completed in accordance with [10 USC 2366] and the report required by [10 USC 2366, subsection (d)] with respect to that testing is submitted. . . . The term "covered system" means a vehicle, weapon, platform, or conventional weapon system—

(A) that includes features designed to provide some degree of protection to users in combat; and

(B) that is a major system [defined as a combination of elements that will function together to produce the capabilities required to fulfill a mission need. The elements may include hardware, equipment, software or any combination thereof, but excludes construction or other improvements to real property]. (10 USC 2366; see also 10 USC 2302)

Descriptions of Activities

Develop, update, or revise annual report of DOT&E (Director, Operational Test and Evaluation). "As part of the annual report of the [Director, Operational Test and Evaluation], the Director shall describe for each program covered in the report the status of test and evaluation activities in comparison with the test and evaluation master plan for that program, as approved by the Director. The Director shall include in such annual report a description of each waiver granted . . . since the last such report" (10 USC 2399, subsection [g]). This activity will collect any effort at the program manager staff level in reviewing applicable portions of the report and providing updated data and programs status.

Review requirements document (please specify document). Principal documents include (but are not limited to) the following:

- Initial Capabilities Document (ICD)
- Capability Development Document (CDD)
- Capability Production Document (CPD).

This activity includes any work done in developing, updating, and clarifying the content of these documents, particularly with respect to how such information affects test planning and requirements. For older programs, please include time spent on Mission Need Statements (MNS) and Operational Requirements Documents (ORDs).

Develop, update, or revise TEMP. This category includes activities related to TEMP (defined earlier).

Develop, update, or revise Beyond LRIP . These are activities related to the Beyond LRIP Report (defined earlier).

Develop, update, or revise operational test plan. As mentioned earlier, one of the following Service organizations responsible for operational test will be responsible for the generation of test plans:

- AFOTEC (Air Force Operational Test and Evaluation Center)
- ATEC (Army Test and Evaluation Command)
- COMOPTEVFOR (Navy Commander, Operational Test and Evaluation Force)
- MCOTEA (Marine Corps Operational Test and Evaluation Activity).

For major defense acquisition programs, DOT&E will review and approve these plans prior to any testing phase (e.g., Operational Assessment, Initial Operational Test & Evaluation, etc.). This activity is intended to capture the program office effort in assisting with test plan development: for example, the work done in collaboration of DT/OT test periods.

Develop, update, or revise LRIP/IOT&E Brief. The purpose of the LRIP effort "is to establish an initial production base for the system, permit an orderly ramp-up sufficient to lead to a smooth transition to [FRP], and to provide production representative articles for [IOT&E] and full-up live fire testing" (*Glossary of Defense Acquisition Acronyms and Terms*, 2003, see DoD Component Acquisition Executive, p. B-82–B-83). IOT&E refers to dedicated OT&E "conducted on production, or production representative articles, to determine whether systems are operationally effective and suitable, and . . . supports the decision to proceed with [BLRIP]" (*Glossary of Defense Acquisition Acronyms and Terms,* 2003, "DoD Component Acquisition Executive," p. B-71).

These two elements form a major portion of the decision process and determination of a program's readiness to proceed beyond Milestone C. This activity is intended to capture the effort in preparing decisionmaking products and collecting information ultimately presented to the MDA for making his or her decision to enter IOT&E utilizing LRIP assets.

Develop, update, or revise FRP Brief. The IOT&E effort "concludes with a Full Rate Production Decision Review (FRPDR) to authorize Full Rate Production and Deployment (FRP&D)" (*Glossary of Defense Acquisition Acronyms and Terms,* 2003, see DoD Component Acquisition Executive, p. B-83). Continuation into full-rate production results from a successful full-rate production decision review by the MDA (or designee). This effort delivers the fully funded quantity of systems and supporting materiel and services for the program or increment to the users. During this effort, units attain Initial Operational Capability. FRP cannot be made until the Operational Test Authority has submitted its final test report after completion of IOT&E. This report will be reviewed by DOT&E, who will complete his or her own final report of testing along with a BLRIP report submitted to Congress, stating that the system is ready for production. This activity is intended to collect the time spent in preparing the necessary data, and build the applicable briefing items for the MDA FRP decision.

Develop, update, or revise Operational Test Readiness Review (OTRR). This encompasses activities related to OTRR (mentioned earlier).

Review live fire test plan/strategy. A "covered system may not proceed beyond low-rate initial production until realistic survivability testing of the system is completed in accordance with [10 USC 2366] and the report . . . with respect to that testing is submitted. . . . [A] major munitions program or a missile program may not proceed beyond low-rate initial production until realistic lethality testing of the program is completed in accordance with [10 USC 2366] and the report . . . with respect to that testing is submitted" (10 USC 2366). DOT&E, along with the program manager's staff, will develop and state in the TEMP the LFT&E plan the number of assets required for testing. If waivers are involved, alternative strategies will be developed to complete testing of the components, subsystems, and subassemblies to determine survivability. This activity will measure the effort in interacting with DOT&E (and other applicable agencies) in developing and executing all aspects of LFT&E with the exception of the waiver process.

Obtain Live Fire Waiver. The Secretary of Defense may waive the application of the survivability and lethality tests for a covered system, munitions program, missile program, or covered product improvement program if the Secretary of Defense, before the system or program enters system development and demonstration, certifies to Congress that live fire testing of such system or that the program would be unreasonably expensive and impractical. In the case of a covered system (or covered product improvement program for a covered system), the Secretary of Defense may waive the application of the survivability and lethality tests for a system or program and instead allow the testing of the system or program in combat by firing munitions likely to be encountered in combat at components, subsystems, and subassemblies, together with performing design analyses, modeling and simulation, and analysis of combat data. This activity is intended to capture the effort of the program office in developing the waiver request and the time spent in processing the waiver request through DOT&E and other agencies.

Other activities related to operational and live fire testing (please specify). Other activities may include significant test-related analysis or related work in preparation for Design Readiness Reviews, software-related T&E and independent verification and validation, and so on. These activities need to be clearly related to T&E issues done in support of MDAP and other major programs.

Bibliography

Acker, David D., *Evaluation of the Effectiveness of the Defense Systems Acquisition Review (DSARC)*, Vol. I: Technical Report with Appendices A and B, Arlington, Va.: Information Spectrum, Inc., April 4, 1983.

Acquisition Reform Cost Savings and Cost Avoidance: A Compilation of Cost Savings and Cost Avoidance Resulting from Implementing Acquisition Reform Initiatives, AFMC draft report, Wright-Patterson AFB, Dayton, Ohio, December 19, 1996.

ADPA—see American Defense Preparedness Association.

American Defense Preparedness Association, *Doing Business with DoD—The Cost Premium*, Washington, D.C., 1992.

Anderson, Michael H., *A Study of the Federal Government's Experiences with Commercial Procurement Practices in Major Defense Acquisitions*, Master's thesis, Cambridge, Mass.: Massachusetts Institute of Technology, June 1997. Online at http://lean.mit.edu/index.php?option=com_docman&task=doc_view&gid=98 (as of May 3, 2006).

Carnegie Commission on Science, Technology, and Government, *A Radical Reform of the Defense Acquisition System*, New York, December 1, 1992.

Center for Strategic and International Studies, *Integrating Commercial and Military Technologies for National Security: An Agenda for Change*, Washington D.C., April 1991.

Chairman of the Joint Chiefs of Staff Instruction (CJCSI) 6212.01B, Interoperability and Supportability of National Security Systems, and Information Technology Systems, May 8, 2000.

——— 3170.01, Operation of the Joint Capabilities Integration and Development System, June 24, 2003.

CJCSI—see Chairman of the Joint Chiefs of Staff Instruction.

Cook, Cynthia R., and John C. Graser, *Military Airframe Acquisition Costs: The Effects of Lean Manufacturing*, Santa Monica, Calif.: RAND Corporation, MR-1325-AF, 2001. Online at http://www.rand.org/pubs/monograph_reports/MR1325/ (as of May 3, 2006).

Coopers & Lybrand, *Acquisition Reform Implementation: An Industry Survey*, report prepared for DoD Service executives, October 1997.

Coopers & Lybrand with TASC, Inc., *The DoD Regulatory Cost Premium: A Quantitative Assessment*, annotated briefing prepared for Secretary of Defense William Perry, December 1994.

CSIS—see Center for Strategic and International Studies.

Defense Policy Panel and Acquisition Policy Panel, House of Representatives Committee on Armed Forces, *Defense Acquisition: Major U.S. Commission Reports (1949–1988)*, Washington, D.C.: U.S. Government Printing Office, 1988.

DoDI—see U.S. Department of Defense Instruction.

Drezner, Jeffrey A., and Giles K. Smith, *An Analysis of Weapon System Acquisition Schedules*, Santa Monica, Calif.: RAND Corporation, R-3937-ACQ, 1990.

Ferrara, Joe, "DoD's 5000 Documents: Evolution and Change in Defense Acquisition Policy," *Acquisition Review Quarterly*, Fall 1996, pp. 109–130. Online at http://www.dau.mil/pubs/arq/94arq/ferrar.pdf (as of May 3, 2006).

GAO—see U.S. General Accounting Office.

Glossary of Defense Acquisition Acronyms and Terms, 11th ed., Fort Belvoir, Va.: Defense Acquisition University Press, September 2003. Online at http://www.jpeocbd.osd.mil/documents/Defense Acroynms.pdf (as of May 3, 2006). Current version (12th ed., July 2005) online at http://www.dau.mil/pubs/glossary/12th_Glossary_2005.pdf (as of May 3, 2006).

Hanks, Christopher H., Elliot I. Axelbrand, Shuna Lindsay, Rehan Malik, and Brett D. Steele, *Reexamining Military Acquisition Reform: Are We There Yet?* Santa Monica, Calif.: RAND Corporation, MG-291-A, 2005. Online at http://www.rand.org/pubs/monographs/MG291/ (as of May 3, 2006).

Honeywell, *Defense Acquisition Improvement Study*, May 1986.

Institute for Defense Analyses, *Role of OSD in the Acquisition Process*, Alexandria, Va., 1991.

Krikorian, George K., "DoD's Cost Premium Thirty to Fifty Percent, National Defense," *Journal of American Defense Preparedness Association*, September 1992.

Lorell, Mark A., and John C. Graser, *An Overview of Acquisition Reform Cost Savings Estimates*, Santa Monica, Calif.: RAND Corporation, MR-1329-AF, 2001. Online at http://www.rand.org/pubs/monograph_reports/MR1329/ (as of May 3, 2006).

Lorell, Mark A., Julia F. Lowell, Michael Kennedy, and Hugh P. Levaux, *Cheaper, Faster, Better? Commercial Approaches to Weapons Acquisition*, Santa Monica, Calif.: RAND Corporation, MR-1147-AF, 2000. Online at http://www.rand.org/pubs/monograph_reports/MR1147/ (as of May 3, 2006).

NORCOM, *Activity-Based Cost Analysis of Cost of DoD Requirements and Cost of Capacity: Executive Summary*, May 1994.

Office of the Assistant Secretary of the Air Force, Acquisition, *Acquisition Reform Success Story: Wind Corrected Munitions Dispenser (WCMD)*, June 12, 1997.

Office of the Deputy Under Secretary of Defense, Acquisition Reform, *Single Process Initiative, Acquisition Reform Acceleration Day Stand-Down*, 1996a.

———, Acquisition Reform, *Cost as an Independent Variable: Stand-Down Acquisition Reform Acceleration Day*, May 1996b.

———, Acquisition Reform, Defense Acquisition Pilot Programs, Pilot Program Consulting Group on Metrics, *Celebrating Success: Forging the Future*, 1997a.

———, Acquisition Reform, Pilot Program Consulting Group, *PPCG 1997 Compendium of Pilot Program Reports*, 1997b.

Office of the Under Secretary of Defense, Acquisition and Technology, *Report of the Defense Science Board Task Force on Acquisition Reform*, Washington, D.C.: Defense Science Board, 1993.

———, Acquisition and Technology, Acquisition Reform Senior Steering Group, DoD Regulatory Cost Premium Group, *Updated Compendium of Office of Primary Responsibility (OPR) Reports*, June 1996.

———, Acquisition and Technology, Acquisition Reform Benchmarking Group, *1997 Final Report*, June 30, 1997.

———, Acquisition and Technology, *Report of the Defense Science Board Task Force on Acquisition Reform, Phase IV*, Washington, D.C.: Defense Science Board, July 1999. Online at http://www.acq.osd.mil/dsb/reports/acqreformfour.pdf (as of May 3, 2006).

OUSD—see Office of the Under Secretary of Defense.

Packard Commission, *Reports of the President's Blue Ribbon Commission on Defense Management, Final Report to the President: A Quest for Excellence*, Washington, D.C., June 1986. Online at http://www.ndu.edu/library/pbrc/pbrc.html (as of May 3, 2006).

Perry, William J., Secretary of Defense, "Acquisition Reform—Mandate for Change," memorandum, February 1994.

———, "Specifications and Standards—A New Way of Doing Business," memorandum, June 29, 1994.

PL—see Public Law.

Public Law 104-106, National Defense Authorization Act for Fiscal Year 1996, 104th Congress, February 10, 1996.

Public Law 107-248, Department of Defense Appropriations Act, 2003, 107th Congress, October 23, 2002.

Rich, Michael, Edmund Dews, and C. L. Batten, *Improving the Military Acquisition Process: Lessons from RAND Research*, Santa Monica, Calif.: RAND Corporation, R-3373-AF/RC, 1986. Online at http://www.rand.org/pubs/reports/R3373/ (as of May 3, 2006).

Rogers, Edward W., and Robert P. Birmingham, "A Ten-Year Review of the Vision for Transforming the Defense Acquisition System," *Defense Acquisition Review Quarterly*, January–April 2004, pp. 36–61. Online at http://www.dau.mil/pubs/arq/2004arq/Rogers.pdf (as of May 3, 2006).

Rush, Benjamin C., "Cost as an Independent Variable: Concepts and Risks," *Acquisition Review Quarterly*, Spring 1997, pp. 161–172. Online at http://www.dau.mil/pubs/arq/97arq/rus.pdf (as of May 3, 2006).

Schank, John, Kathi Webb, Eugene Bryton, and Jerry Sollinger, *Analysis of Service-Reported Acquisition Reform Reductions: An Annotated Briefing*, Santa Monica, Calif.: RAND Corporation, unpublished research, September 1996.

Secretary of the Navy Instruction (SECNAVINST) 5000.2B, Implementation of Mandatory Procedures for Major and Non-Major Defense Acquisition Programs and Major and Non-Major Information Technology Acquisition Programs, December 6, 1996.

Smith, Giles K., Jeffrey A. Drezner, William C. Martel, James J. Milanese, W. E. Mooz, and E. C. River, *A Preliminary Perspective on Regulatory Activities and Effects in Weapons Acquisition*, Santa Monica, Calif.: RAND Corporation, R-3578-ACQ, 1988.

Sylvester, Richard K., and Joseph A. Ferrara, "Conflict and Ambiguity: Implementing Evolutionary Acquisition," *Acquisition Review Quarterly*, Winter 2003. Online at http://www.dau.mil/pubs/arq/2003arq/Sylvesterwt3.pdf (as of May 3, 2006).

USC—see U.S. Code.

United States Code, Title 10, Armed Forces, Chapter 4, Office of the Secretary of Defense, Section 139, Director of Operational Test and Evaluation, January 19, 2004.

———, Title 10, Armed Forces, Chapter 137, Procurement Generally, Section 2302, Definitions, January 19, 2004.

———, Title 10, Armed Forces, Chapter 139, Research and Development, Section 2366, Major Systems and Munitions Programs: Survivability, Testing and Lethality Testing Required Before Full-Scale Production, January 19, 2004.

———, Title 10, Armed Forces, Chapter 141, Miscellaneous Procurement Provisions, Section 2399, Operational Test and Evaluation of Defense Acquisition Programs, January 19, 2004.

———, Title 10, Armed Forces, Chapter 144, Major Defense Acquisition Programs, Section 2440, Technology and Industrial Base Plans, January 19, 2004.

———, Title 10, Armed Forces, Chapter 146, Contracting for Performance of Civilian Commercial or Industrial Type Functions, Section 2464, Core Logistics Capabilities, January 19, 2004.

———, Title 10, Armed Forces, Chapter 146, Contracting for Performance of Civilian Commercial or Industrial Type Functions, Section 2466, Limitations on the Performance of Depot-Level Maintenance of Materiel, January 19, 2004.

U.S. Congress, House of Representatives Committee on Armed Forces, *Future of the Defense Industrial Base: Report of the Structure of the U.S. Defense Industrial Base Panel*, 1992.

U.S Congress, Office of Technology Assessment, *Holding the Edge: Maintaining the Defense Technology Base, Volume 2: Appendixes*, Washington D.C.: U.S. Government Printing Office, OTA-ISC-432, April 1989.

———, *Redesigning Defense: Planning the Transition to the Future U.S. Defense Industrial Base*, Washington, D.C.: U.S. Government Printing Office, OTA-ISC-500, July 1991.

U.S. Department of Defense, *The Defense Transformation for the 21st Century*, Washington, D.C.: General Council of the Department of Defense, April 10, 2003. Online at http://www.oft.osd.mil/library/library_files/document_131_Dod%20Transformation%20Act%20.pdf (as of May 3, 2006).

———, *Report of the Defense Science Board Task Force on Management Oversight in Acquisition Organizations*, Washington, D.C.: Office of the Under Secretary of Defense for Acquisition, Technology, and Logistics, March 2005. Online at http://www.acq.osd.mil/dsb/reports/2005-03-MOAO_Report_Final.pdf (as of May 3, 2006).

U.S. Department of Defense Directive (DoDD) 5000.1, The Defense Acquisition System, May 12, 2003.

U.S. Department of Defense, Defense Systems Management College, *Streamlining Defense Acquisition Laws, Executive Summary: Report of the DoD Acquisition Law Advisory Panel*, Fort Belvoir, Va.: Defense Systems Management College Press, March 1993.

U.S. Department of Defense Instruction (DoDI) 5000.2, Operation of the Defense Acquisition System, May 12, 2003.

U.S. General Accounting Office, *Acquisition Reform: Efforts to Reduce the Cost to Manage and Oversee DoD Contracts*, report to congressional committees, Washington, D.C., GAO/NSIAD-96-106, April 1996. Online at http://www.gao.gov/archive/1996/ns96106.pdf (as of May 3, 2006).

———, *Acquisition Reform: DoD Faces Challenges in Reducing Oversight Costs*, report to congressional committees, Washington, D.C., GAO/NSIAD-97-48, January 1997a. Online at http://www.gao.gov/archive/1997/ns97048.pdf (as of May 3, 2006).

———, *Acquisition Reform: Effect on Weapon System Funding*, report to the Secretary of Defense, Washington, D.C., GAO/NSIAD-98-31, October 1997b. Online at http://www.gao.gov/archive/1998/ns98031.pdf (as of May 3, 2006).